TESTIMONIES

DATE DUE

MAR 1 2 1997	
MAR 2 5 1997	
OCT 1 5 1997	
OCT 2 9 1997	
DEC - 2 1997	
APR 2 9 1999	

BRODART   Cat. No. 23-221

Testimonies

Lesbian Coming-Out Stories

edited by
Karen Barber & Sarah Holmes

Boston ◆ Alyson Publications, Inc.

Published as a trade paperback original by Alyson Publications, Inc.,
40 Plympton Street, Boston, Massachusetts 02118.
Distributed in England by GMP Publishers,
P.O. Box 247, London N17 9QR, England.

An earlier version of Nancy Wechsler's essay, "Front-Page News,"
was published in *Gay Community News,* vol. 11, no. 49.

First edition: October 1988
Second edition: January 1994

ISBN 1-55583-245-8

5   4   3   2   1

Contents

Introduction

The coming-out story has no parallel in heterosexual culture. The ritual of telling others, in print or in person, "when I knew," "who I told," and "what I did" is unique to lesbian, gay, and bisexual culture, and a tradition within our community. Each story told becomes a part of our community's history, reminding us how times have changed, or as the case may be, how much things have stayed the same.

Now is a wonderfully exciting time to be coming out. The 1990s have brought tremendous visibility to lesbians; *Time, Glamour,* even *Cosmopolitan* have run features on us. And though these stories are often superficial and sensationalistic, they have made information about lesbians accessible to everyone, whether in San Francisco or in Boise. And when a scared, young lesbian sees two women hugging on the cover of *Newsweek* — each time she sees the word *lesbian* in print — she is no longer isolated; she is no longer alone. I hope that *Testimonies,* too, finds its way into the hands of women who are searching for validation of their desires, hungry for words and images that reflect their lives and their truths.

Of course, with advancement comes backlash. We don't have to look any further than Colorado's or Oregon's anti-gay referendums to see that life as lesbians still isn't always easy. But even in the face of political harassment, job discrimination, and familial condemnation, being true to yourself is the best option for a happy life. This doesn't necessarily mean pro-

---

claiming your lesbianism from the rooftops; deciding when and where to come out is a personal choice. But, as lesbians, we need to fight our way through the societal lies and the anti-gay propaganda and accept ourselves and those we love as people worthy of everything this world has to offer.

Sarah Holmes compiled the first edition of *Testimonies* in 1988. For this new edition, we worked together to find new lesbian voices to share. This book represents just a small fraction of the millions of coming-out stories that could be told. I hope that every dyke who reads this book will find something with which she can identify. We're all different, and we all come to our lesbianism from different histories. Some of us always knew we were gay, and others have come out as grandmothers. Some of us have been married; others have never been with men. What's important is finally realizing that we can love women, feel good about it, and know that there are many others who feel the same way.

—Karen Barber

TESTIMONIES

Sally Miller Gearhart

Small-Town Girl Makes Dyke

Miss Zella Woodrum (Miss Zudie) and Miz Maude Caroline Puckett Miller swung back and forth in their rockers in front of Miss Zudie's fire. "I declare, Miss Zudie," said Maude Caroline in a low voice (convinced that since I was in the bathroom, I would not hear her), "the day Frank Miller died was the day my life began!"

"Is that so!" Miss Zudie reached across the hassock that sat between them and touched my grandmother's arm. "Well, Miss Maude, they all say that life begins at forty!"

My grandmother responded with words I could not distinguish, and the two women collapsed into rolls of laughter, rocking and nodding and embellishing the conversation with further low-spoken comments.

We were in the midst of our weekly visit to Miss Zudie's (to be paralleled in three days' time by her weekly visit to our house), precious pastime, sacred rituals. The only thing that could have threatened these intensely anticipated occasions might have been a spontaneous bridge game, for in the '30s, Pearisburg (pronounced "Parisburg") citizens lived each day fixated on bingo, radio, or bridge. But Miss Maudie had very deliberately disciplined herself on this matter: she played bridge regularly two nights a week and at the drop of a hat, *except* on the evenings that she and Miss Zudie were to get together. Nothing, not even the eventual advent of duplicate bridge in our town, ever kept Maude Miller away from her visits with Miss Zella Woodrum.

I liked it best when we were the visitors. Maudie would bundle me up in my leggings – or if it was summer she'd hand me my sweater – grab her knitting, and up the street we'd go to the rambling old grey house on the corner. Maybe we'd sit in front Miss Zudie's stove in the kitchen, where the walls were papered with calendars in exact order back to 1887 and where hundreds of small and large empty matchboxes were neatly stacked on every available shelf surface or windowsill. Miss Zudie never threw anything away. Usually she meticulously wrapped it and gave it a label. Once, in my explorations of the old house, I discovered a small box marked "Strings Too Short To Use." Inside were strings. Too short to use.

Or maybe the two women would sit in front of the fireplace in Miss Zudie's cozy bedroom. I was the needle-threader and, when there was yarn to be rolled up, official skein-holder. Miss Zudie always saw to the tea or coffee or warm cider, and Maudie would make a big ceremony out of cutting yarn or thread with the penknife she carried forever in her pocket-book, a gift to her from me and Miss Zudie. "Comes in so handy for so many things!" she'd exclaim. "The other day I used it to cut back that forsythia bush."

In warm weather the two women sat in wicker chairs under the big maples in Miss Zudie's weed-high yard. They swatted at gnats and sipped lemonade and meandered from subject to subject and back again. I remember most vividly their absorption with genealogy – what was the name of Yance Peters's second boy, who had married the Woolwine girl from Clover

Hollow and did that or did that not make Ola Brotherton and Bess Pasterfield second-cousins-once-removed? And with propriety — how Miss Maudie's relatives out on Curve Road still butchered the King's English, saying "hadda went," "coulda took," "ought to have saw," and "like to have fell."

Whatever the season, wherever they were, and whatever those two talked about, I loved to lean against Maudie's legs and just let their voices roll over me. Vocal caresses, intimate and warm, always punctuated by the formal "Miss Zudie" and "Miss Maude."

Sometimes one of them would say, "Why don't you go on out and talk to Mr. Bill?" Reluctantly I'd relocate to the front porch, where Miss Zudie's brother watched the town go by from his high perch above the street. Mr. Bill, like Miss Zudie, had never married, but unlike her, he rarely socialized. He could lay a plash of tobacco juice right between your toes with the accuracy of a sharpshooter, and he carved wonderful ornate bedposts from cherry wood. I figured he had things to teach me.

Just after her death nearly forty years later, I found among my grandmother's things a faintly scented packet of letters from Miss Zudie, written when she made her yearly visit down to Clintwood. In one of them she had written, "Oh, how I long to get home again and to hear you coming up the path to my kitchen door. The sound of your footsteps sets my heart to pounding!"

Until I came along, Maude Miller was the only woman of the Puckett-Miller clan to "get educated." She'd earned a teaching degree in 1901 at Martha Washington, a women's college. The temper of her steel was truly tested in 1929, when my grandfather died and the Great Depression descended on our Appalachian town. Maudie didn't drop a stitch. She turned down four would-be husbands that I was aware of (and probably more), converted our home into a rooming house, took up teaching high school (yearly salary: $100), and embarked on a life that ultimately earned her the reputation of a town character.

She fired her own furnace, rebuilt her own kitchen, remained the only Republican in a fiercely Democratic family, got "churched" for playing bridge on Sunday, and mowed her own grass (once, I remember, at midnight, while I held the flashlight and she recited "The Charge of the Light Brigade"). She learned to drive at sixty-five and characteristically drove in the middle of the street, trusting that any policeman who apprehended her — or any judge who tried her case — would be either one of her past students or blood kin, neither of whom would do more than reprimand Miz Miller/Aunt Maude.

I went back to Pearisburg in 1974 to see my family. When Maudie heard me drive up, she leapt out of her chair with excitement, for we hadn't seen each other in four years. In that moment, she fell and broke her hip, a condition to which her active spirit was never reconciled. She died alone in a nursing home within the year.

It is not true, as the folks in town say, that she died in triumph playing a seven-no-trump hand. But it is true that there were two things on her bedside table: an old penknife and a deck of cards.

◆

When my mother (Maudie's daughter) was a child, she and her best friend were inseparable. In the warm summers when nightfall overtook them in their play, my mother, Sarah Elizabeth, called "Dit," would protectively walk Phoebe home over the four blocks between their houses. Then Phoebe would walk Dit home so she wouldn't be scared. And, of course, Dit would have to walk Phoebe home again. I picture them giggling and holding hands, swinging up and down the maple-lined streets of Pearisburg, far into the magic evenings.

They were once in a play together where one of them (they could never remember which one) was named "Miss Laurie." For the rest of their lives, through marriages, children, separations, depression, death, family scandals, and genteel poverty, the two women called each other "Miss Laurie," still visiting regularly, still exchanging birthday and Christmas gifts, still talking long hours on the phone. My mother's death ended their seventy-year friendship, and until she herself died, Miss Phoebe placed flowers on Miss Dit's grave every August 10th, her birthday.

The Crash of 1929 had catapulted Miss Dit out of her only year in college and into the arms of my handsome, drinking, gambling, womanizing, reprobate father. Her divorce from him when I was two was unheard of, because, once married, the women of Pearisburg stayed that way, often simply enduring a grim fate. It was the first divorce in the county's history. With no skills and a child to support, Dit moved to Richmond, 250 miles away, to learn typing and shorthand at night while she worked by day as a stenographer in the Home Owners' Loan Corporation, one of FDR's antidotes to the failed national economy.

I lived with her in Richmond until I was school-age, cared for by Katherine Summers, the black woman who had escaped Pearisburg with Dit and who ultimately found work and love and a family in Richmond. The boardinghouse at three-oh-two West Franklin Street (an address I was drilled on lest I become lost in the city) was run by Mrs. Hardaway and her daughter. It was peopled by single or divorced women, who, like my mother, had come from all over the state to find jobs. Dit and I shared a bedroom with two other women, warm happy souls who played cards and dominos with me.

I loved my times with Katherine, spent mostly in the kitchen with Susie, the cook, or out in Monroe Park's sandbox — where Chucky Klotz once called me a sissy for having a doll. That resulted in my first full-fledged fight, one I have always believed I won, though Katherine (whom I still visit in Richmond even after these fifty-odd years) has a different notion of the encounter.

Fun though the park was, I always looked forward to six o'clock, when most of the women came home to strip off their uniforms or wiggle out of their corsets and hose and tight shoes. I would sit on the stairs between the second and third floors and listen to them sighing with relief and calling out to one another the excitements of the day, the contentments of at last being home. I remember dinnertime as a loud affair, full of boisterous conversation and laughter, tales of woe, and teasings about boyfriends — who never, somehow, materialized on the premises.

Three-oh-two was a house of women. Even after her return to Pearisburg many years later, my mother kept up correspondence and visits with her friends there, and she told me just before she died that those years in Richmond in that boardinghouse, those hard-times-of-the-Great-Depression, had actually been the freest and happiest days of her adult life.

◆

After I started school back in Pearisburg, I could only visit my mother, my Katherine, and my Richmond boardinghouse during summertime, when Maudie would take me on the Norfolk and Western's Powhatan Arrow from Ripplemead down through the low mountain passes and winding rivers to the flatlands of eastern Virginia. In other seasons I was exploring caves or mountaintops with the 4-H Club, playing kick-the-can in the fresh spring nights, swinging from grapevines, falling from trees, coasting down long white winter hills, or (with "the girls") defending snow or stickweed forts against "the boys," on whom we had early on declared war and with whom we seemed constantly to be in physical fights that cost us our lunch hours and our recesses.

The companion of many of my days was Wanza, five years my senior, and so "high yeller" that we were often mistaken for sisters. Wanza's job for the six years we were together was to keep me out of trouble while Maudie conducted her affairs of school and rooming house. Wanza taught me to cuss, rassle, box, play mumblety-peg, put English on my steelies so I could be a marbles champion, and sail a stickweed straight and far. Best of all, when we went to the movies I'd get to sit with her in the balcony with the black folks, where the most fun always was and where the best commentary on the film always took place.

And Wanza taught me to run, coaching me on how to conserve my breath — how to breathe solely through my nose at first and then, after the big exhaustion came, how to capture the miracle of second wind. Wanza ran everywhere — to work, to school, to the grocery store, to the sinkhole, up and down the big hill to Bluff City — and when she was sixteen, she ran straight to the big heart and ample arms of Bob Bleddins, one of the town's derelicts, whom Wanza's mama was for some reason ashamed for her to associate with. I only later realized Wanza was shacking up with him.

So we sometimes hung out with Bob, always on the sly and with me sworn not to tell Wanza's mama. Though he taught me some of the subtleties of crapshooting, I remember some-times being jealous of Wanza's attentions to this man. More than twenty-five years later, when I was taking her to Roanoke for her operation for throat cancer, I confessed that jealousy to her. "Pshaw!" Wanza sputtered. "That man meant shit to me, don't you know that? Just company, that's all." Then she fixed me with those soft brown eyes. "It was you and me, that's who," she said. "You and me, to kingdom come. Right?"

Wanza died the following year. I wasn't there to see her ushered into heaven, but I'm sure she went in running.

◆

The text of my childhood was the patriarchal one: men are the more important sex; they have the information, the skills, the tools, the opportunities, and the say-so; women participate in knowledge and power only through men. That text was articulated for me by movies, schools, churches, newspapers, books, magazines, and radio programs; certainly I saw it at work in the social structures of my small town and in the big city of Richmond.

Yet the unspoken message of my days, the subtext of my childhood, was a different one: *Men do not matter*. No voice spoke those words, no headline announced it, no sermon suggested it. The women who surrounded me simply lived their lives as if men were, though occasionally nice or some-times interesting, basically insignificant. Women, they seemed to say, are the source of power, the heart of the action, the focal point of love. Women trust, honor, and enjoy one another.

That subtext became a fundamental part of my worldview, sustaining me in rough times and firing in me a tremendous creative energy; more recently it has granted me hope that the earth can be restored, that all its creatures can regain their sanity, health, freedom, and dignity.

Though most of the women of Pearisburg and those of the Richmond boardinghouse would be offended to be called lesbians, in my experience, they differ from lesbians only in their lack of sexual experience with other women. Granted, that's a *significant* lack, but it is not a *signifying* lack. Certainly sexual love with another woman can transform the quality of a woman's every subsequent behavior or attitude. But other acts between women may be equally transformative. We all know women who call themselves lesbians but who have not yet had a sexual experience with another woman. We also know women who have had sexual experiences with other women who identify as heterosexual. I've decided that though sex has enhanced my lesbianism and empowered my womanness, it hasn't in itself made me a lesbian.

Still, the words *lesbian* or *gay* or *homosexual* and the myths and stereotypes that attended these words, struck fear into the hearts of the women of my hometown. When I told my mother that I was a lesbian, her response was "Can you get an operation?" When I told my grandmother, she became "sick to the ends of my toes," because I was something "unnatural." Katherine Summers, a pillar of the African Methodist Episcopal Zion Church, said, after a long silence, "I love you anyway." Miss Phoebe's daughter changed the subject. Wanza was the sole exception to the experience: she grinned and said, "No shit." Even after the advent of the women's movement, even now in these days of open discussion and debate, the words are highly charged.

I've often asked myself over these past two decades why families, friends, co-workers, acquaintances, even strangers, still have such trouble handling our coming out as lesbians.

Certainly our saying who we are identifies the previously ignored hippopotamus in the living room and forces those we tell to deal with our "sin" or "sickness." And certainly by coming out we offend any narrow view of sexuality or rigid religious dogma. Politically, of course, our coming out threatens patriarchy and the nuclear family — we aren't behaving like regular girls, fussing over men, marrying them, having *their* babies.

I am convinced, though, that the women I grew up with had (or would have had) such an extreme and negative reaction to my coming out not because they thought I was damned or evil or sick or flying in the face of God's laws. They froze and trembled and cried and said, "Sh-h-h-h!" because my coming out was too close to home, because their own lives were testimonies to precisely the "abomination" I was proudly claiming for myself. Perhaps by announcing it so loudly, by trying to make their subtext into a text, I threatened the security of their world in a way they did not consciously recognize.

In 1972 I went to New York to be on Tom Snyder's *Tomorrow* show, where three other women and I discussed our pride and our joy at being lesbians. Pearisburg, Virginia, of course had its late-night viewers, and by noon the following day (I'm told by still-closeted gay sources there), the news was all over town that Sally Miller Gearhart was on national television "being a homosexual." All over town, that is, except to the ears of my mother and grandmother. It's a testimony, I guess, to what they would consider their good taste or their respect for my family that even good friends of my folks never told them of my appearance on that show. In fact, I had already come out to my mother and grandmother. So there was the town protecting my family from what it thought they didn't know, and there was my family, knowing the dark secret but not knowing that everyone else knew.

I like to think that in some part of themselves the women in my hometown who heard about or saw that show — Wanza, Miss Zudie, Miss Phoebe and her daughter, my old piano teacher, my old English teacher, three or four nurses at the hospital, a lot of the girls I went to school with, my mother's co-workers, some of my grandmother's bridge partners — knew that my joy and pride in loving other women was at least in part a legacy from them and from the women of my family, that what I was saying to them was a simple "Thank you." I like to think that they then nodded to me an equally simple "You're welcome."

Nona Caspers

Home

For me there was no one clinching moment, mad love, or political leap that landed me in Lesbos. Coming out to myself and to others was a matter of finding a way to survive and letting myself thrive.

I was one of those wispy white-haired girls, born into rural Minnesota, Catholicism, and the '60s. My strong legs were wrapped in itchy pink tights and hidden under synthetic frills. I remember twirling round and round in the driveway, with my long hair flying, and skirts flapping like feminine flags. I was happy. I had a neighborhood full of Catholic girlfriends. We played SPUD, Annie Annie Over, Wonder Bread Communion, Chinese Sticks, dolls, and another game we called Tickle. We would climb four at a time, one on each pole of a swingset, mishmashing our vulvas against the metal until a tickle rooted between our legs and sprouted throughout our blessed bodies. We giggled and talked to each other the whole time. Vicky, Beth, or Lisa's face hung across from mine. It was an intimate, soothing, and sacred girl ritual.

Then there was Romeo and Juliet — we took turns being one or the other. We held hands and kissed, passionately twisting our lips together like Steve and Rachel on *Another World*. I remember the times we slept at each other's houses, and cuddled up close like two chips melting together. And we'd talk; intense, excited talk that mixed our thoughts and feelings together like dough.

I felt safe and warm during those years. The closeness, these friendships were what life was all about. Nobody said anything to me about the touching. We were just little girls playing.

By the seventh grade, with breasts and blood approaching, my childhood safety had disappeared. In my rural high school, the "sexual revolution" meant girls felt more pressure, called freedom, to revolve around the penis. While the Church encouraged my "safe" friendships with girls, the coolest, bravest deed was to touch a boy. I started to hang out with the most heterosexually active girls. We would sit nose to nose, knee to knee, whispering, with my long hair floating between our intense faces. Our words and voices mingled, rose and fell. Our closeness depended on telling every detail. I had nothing to tell. Certain boys made me nervous, and I took these feelings to be crushes. But I would rather be with my girlfriends talking about it than with those boys, doing something about it — and for all their boy-crazy activity, they did too.

As the pressure increased, I became extremely anxious. I began to sense that there was something wrong with me. Not the usual zit on the tip of my nose or the "tell-me-the-truth-am-I-weird" insecurities of adolescence. I felt a cold white secret, a longing, lodged beneath my rib cage. I had to guard this spot from everyone, even myself. I acted like a tough femme — seductive, confident. I entertained my girlfriends by getting into trouble; sassing at teachers, running loud, wild, and bold. I remember sneaking apples from a yard we passed during our daily phys. ed. run and giving them to my newest close friend, Carrie. Teachers kicked me out of classes and told me to "act like a lady." Although my girlfriends admired my guts, I felt scared every minute of every day, as though at any time some filth would spill out of me, rolling and clanging on the streets for everyone to see. The only part I could name was the fear.

I became preoccupied with trying to figure out how I would ever be in a heterosexual relationship as there seemed to be no other kind. The intimacy and emotional attachments with girlfriends, and, later, women friends, came so easily and felt so natural and fulfilling. Intimacy felt so impossible, so utterly out of reach and dangerous with men. Yet, in the world I grew up in, heterosexuality was inevitable. The only women I had ever known that got out of it were nuns. I did *not* want to be a nun.

I remember two isolated and very buried incidents in my teen years, when my emotional attractions became sexualized. Carrie invited me over to her house, seven miles from my hometown of Melrose, Minnesota. I remember being very excited. I dressed carefully, brushed my long, blonde hair until the brush bristles sagged, and accentuated my breasts. I thought of her breasts, how they had popped out and were so fleshy and firm. A hope dug its way to the surface of my thoughts, with a vague wish that something might happen and Carrie might want to play.

We were sitting in her older sister's car, going through her purse, when we found a flat round pillbox with the days of the week printed on it. Carrie asked me if I knew what they were. I did. We sat quiet a long time, and the air thickened. Then she asked me if I wanted to play a boy-girl game. I acted dumb and said, "Sure," praying to the Catholic God I'd grown up with that she meant what I thought. She did. I remember clearly how our bodies folded so comfortably together. I felt warm and safe — like home. I thought it couldn't last. It could only be practice for the real thing. We were just playing.

The next time we were sexual was two years later. As she invited me, she said that she knew two boys, Kenny and Bob, who would meet us at a cafe. I was anxious and felt sick, but I wanted to be with her, to talk and talk and laugh into the night. My stomach pains went away when the boys didn't show up and we returned to her house. Finally, we lay in bed and I pretended to be asleep. My skin tingled as I wished that she would touch me. She did. I stayed half asleep, not daring to respond as she moved my hands over her breasts. I mumbled, "Kenny"; she whispered, "Bob." In the morning we could not look each other in the eye. We both said, "I had a dream about a boy."

Soon after this dream, I made a few drugged, drunken attempts to connect with the other gender. Boys liked me, but I didn't seem to care about them. I retreated into starvation and obsessive exercise. I whittled away my female flesh, my anger, my fears, my sexuality. My goal in life was to be able to wear my twelve-year-old brother's Levi's. I did. I was sixteen.

When I was twenty-one, I was hiding two things — my eating patterns and my virginity. At times, I lied. I had avoided contact with men as much as possible, continuing to seek out close women friends wherever I went. But enough was enough, I told myself. If I could hike alone through Guatemala, climb volcanos, live in a teepee and out of a van, put up eleven cords of wood, and get A's in chemistry, then surely I could develop a "normal" emotional and sexual relationship with a nice man.

I picked Doc. We were both planting trees in the South. He turned out to be gay, or "bisexual with a heavy emotional inclination toward men." After our first bout of intercourse, he asked me if I was a lesbian. I laughed and said, "No," with confidence.

Lesbians were somebody else. Lesbians were the women in the lesbian section of *Our Bodies, Ourselves* — women with short hair and caps, standing together with arms across shoulders, hands cupping each other's breasts — those were lesbians. The scenes in *Going Down with Janice,* Peggy Castenada's unscrupulous book, which I read secretly in high school — that was lesbianism. Kim, a girl in high school who carved her name into her arm and gifted me with stolen incense burners before she ran off to California, and then called me up and told me she had a wife — she was a lesbian. A lesbian was a woman who had sex with women, who craved sex with women, who creamed her jeans whenever she was with women — I didn't; I wasn't. I creamed my jeans for no one.

Ironically, I held some admiration, awe, and respect for lesbians. As an ex-Catholic, I held onto the feeling that somehow it was better to fool around with women than to be defiled by men. Being lesbian was close to being a nun. Lesbians were different; sometimes, they looked comfortable, playful, happy, and independent. At other times, I saw them as fad hoppers, immature and ill. Mostly, I didn't think of them at all, and neither did anyone else I knew.

I decided I had found love with Doc. I nurtured and protected my fantasy of being with him, not caring that he had "emotional homosexual tendencies." There was nothing wrong with that. But whenever I was with him, I felt lonely, irritable, and needy. My eating patterns got worse. I was exhausted and cold. I thought that all I needed, for my sanity and to fulfill my heterosexual fantasy, was to get well.

I moved to Minneapolis, Minnesota, and began to attend a women's eating-disorder group. The women in the group were creative, independent, and also afraid. Soon after joining the group, I caught on that half of them were lesbians. I had dinner at a couple's house and saw how loving and how "normal" they were. In the group, we talked more and more about how our food problems related to being female in a female-hating world. We were being controlled through myths and values about weight. Our energy to create, question, and fight back was drained or diffused by our focus on food and the constant public reference to our bodies and our appearance. We talked about the cycle of starving and binging as an escape from the expectations put upon traditional femininity. Then I made a very special friend, Julie.

Julie was never my lover, but she was the first woman I thought about being lovers with. She was a real girlfriend, and together we explored the idea that we could, if we wanted to, be lesbians.

Gradually, as I became familiar with more lesbians and aware that a lesbian culture did exist, I began remembering and understanding my childhood and adolescence. And I began to relax. There was a place for me. I did not have to force myself to be with men. I was lesbian. I was home.

I have identified myself as a lesbian for five years. I have been "well" for about that long. I was in a relationship for two years and am now preparing to date. The first time my ex-sweetheart and I played was like a warm, safe trip into a time when I was whole. Everyone in my ten-person German Catholic family knows. When I recently told my still-Catholic sister, with my heart pounding, she smiled and said, "I was wondering if you were ever going to tell me."

*Alana Corsini**

Loving Jenny

We met during our first year of college. There were four of us; four young women who wanted to be actresses, writers, painters, or dancers. We were at college during the Vietnam era, and while we were politically and socially involved in our times, it was our shared artistic dream that bound us together. Surprisingly, twenty years later, we have all achieved a version of our early dreams. Jenny and Tilly are actresses who work in television and film in Los Angeles, Mona is a Bay Area painter with regular shows, and I spend a lot of time at my word processor in New York spewing forth novels, poems, plays, screenplays, and articles on the arts.

No self-respecting aspiring artist or intellectual joined sororities in those days, so the four of us rented an old "railroad" apartment a mile from campus. It had three bedrooms and a glassed-in front porch, which allowed each of us to have a private room. The wallpaper in the dining room featured a grey feather motif against a bland background the color of an internal organ, and the living room couch was supported on one side with empty coffee cans filled with pebbles. It was heaven. I claimed the large bedroom, which could accommo-

---

* A penname has been used to assure the author's anonymity.

date my double bed, covered with an obligatory Indian-print bedspread. I had a huge slate-top desk; a bookcase filled with poetry and esoteric, occult philosophy; and an ancient radiator spray-painted a dull gold. I thought the room struck just the right note between intellectual and erotic.

The late '60s and early '70s was touted as an era of great sexual freedom, although this freedom was bounded by the presumption of heterosexuality. Given that one provision, anything else was acceptable. Mona fell in love with the graduate student upstairs, and lived with him for years before they married. Tilly went in for serial monogamy. Sex was something she fit in between rehearsals, callbacks, and career planning.

Jenny and I, however, entered the sexual Olympics with great vigor during our college years. It required the skills of an air traffic controller to orchestrate the comings and goings of our various lovers. Jenny ran the gamut from a sweet, stuttering fraternity boy to an Italian rock musician she met in Milan to a middle-aged millionaire playboy. I did my part with a bisexual actor, assorted professors (I was an intellectual groupie), a rotund hospital administrator, and an angelic theological student who, in the grip of illicit sex, was losing faith.

Homosexuality to me, at that time, was associated with ancient Greece, modern French literature, and one openly gay Arab actor I knew in school. As far as it pertained to women, I knew about Gertrude Stein, tough dykes in motorcycle jackets, and Colette's experiences in boarding school. And I considered myself sophisticated.

When we graduated in 1971, our core of four dissolved. Only Jenny and I got degrees — Mona was already off with Ron at another university, and Tilly had dropped out to take up a great career opportunity and got married quickly and quietly to her first husband.

I went off to New York to work for a peace/environmental agency by day and an off-Broadway producer by night. It was a lonely year. I had two or three affairs with men I didn't care about, and yearned for the closeness I had had with friends. Jenny was with an improvisational comedy troupe, and we corresponded constantly by letter and tape. Through the months, our exchanges became tinged with longing, loss, and a feeling that in our new lives no one knew us as authentically as we knew each other.

After a year in New York, I impulsively decided to move to Hawaii with two male friends from college and passed through Chicago to say good-bye to my family and whatever friends were still around. I had a strong need to see Jenny and arranged to spend a week with her before leaving for my Pacific adventure.

During the seven-hour drive, I found myself in a state of nervous excitement, belting out torch songs Jenny and I used to sing in college. It was to be a homecoming and an adventure all in one. Jenny. I hadn't seen her in almost a year and there was nobody I wanted to see more.

Jenny was living in an apartment in an old white frame house with a roommate named Karen, an actress and auto mechanic who carried her own set of VW tools wherever she traveled as a sort of insurance policy against the vicissitudes of theatrical life. When I arrived, Jenny was alone in the apartment, and I was happy for the rare opportunity to have her to myself. She was a Leo and a born entertainer, and tended to gather crowds around her.

At six feet, Jenny had a flair for theatrical costume. She concocted outfits from thrift-shop castoffs, strings of beads, and scarfs that suggested a moving caravan. Other times, she'd wear a military or pea coat and stocking cap to create an image of Verushka playing Billy Budd. This day, she stood before me unadorned, wearing plain blue slacks and an Oxford-cloth shirt. Her blonde hair – which had been rinsed a unique orange-pink shade during her summer modeling in Italy and only now was halfway returned to its natural color – was shorn close to her head. Mannish, I thought, and felt a lurch in my stomach as we hugged and held each other close for a long moment.

We were both physical people – huggers and embracers and touchers – but for the first time there was awkwardness between us. It must have been the long separation, I thought fleetingly. Then we plunged into our stories over countless cups of coffee, and all strangeness vanished. We knew each other. We loved each other. We had years of shared crisis and jubilation and insight and growing up in common. Everything would be fine, I thought.

But it wasn't. The strangeness returned; the strain in the air, the uncomfortable silences. For two days I followed Jenny around in her life. Was it my imagination, or did she purposely keep other people near us most of the time? I went to rehearsals with her. We ate most meals with the other actors, and Jenny had the troupe over to the apartment both nights. There was singing and good humor and rarely a private moment.

Finally, very late and long after Karen had gone to bed, Jenny and I would tumble into her bedroom and drop, exhausted, onto her waterbed and fall asleep. Although I had never seen her room before, it felt familiar. She had the wire sculpture from her college room on the wall opposite the bed, and strings of beads and baubles were looped over chairs and racks. I was conscious of keeping my body from touching Jenny as we slept, not wanting to ... to what?

I was miserable. Jenny would start to give me a delicious massage on the undulating waterbed, then abruptly jump up to make coffee. Or she'd draw me a hot bubble bath and call me into the bathroom, only to avert her eyes and rush out of the room when I slipped into the water. Something was definitely wrong.

On the third day, Jenny left at midmorning for rehearsal and asked me to meet her at the local pizza parlor for lunch. I lay around most of the morning reading poetry and writing in my journal in an effort to figure out exactly what was going on. I was off to Hawaii on a great adventure, but how come I wasn't thrilled and raring to get going? I decided that it was useless to hang around with Jenny any longer. Maybe now that we were out of college we didn't have that much in common anymore. She was so involved with the theater and her actor friends, there didn't seem to be much room for me. Sharing a past doesn't guarantee a continued closeness, I reasoned. I'd just tell Jenny at lunch that I needed to get a lot of things cleared up in Chicago before I left, and that I couldn't stay the entire week as I had originally planned. She'd understand. We'd always be friends and keep in touch.

Once the decision was made, my mood took a decided turn for the better. I gathered my books together and packed my bag before I started out for the restaurant. I smiled and hummed a tune as I strolled down the street. For the first time, I was aware of the delicate intricacies of the tree branches above me.

When I arrived, Jenny was sitting alone in the corner, resting her elbows on the edge of a table covered with a red-checked cloth. I sat down, brimming with my newly found good humor, and ordered pizza and a Coke. I felt light and at ease and chatted a good deal about nothing in particular.

Jenny's face started to brighten. She commented on how I seemed like my old self once again and laughed in her easy, generous way. I was about to tell her that I was leaving that afternoon when I caught the sudden intensity of her gaze. The smile gently faded from Jenny's face. Our eyes locked on each other, and my heart turned over in my chest. I recognized the look in Jenny's luminous brown eyes and the hot feeling coursing through my body. Desire. We both felt it. And we both knew it.

To this day, I don't remember who spoke first, but I remember the simple question: "Do you want to go?" Knives and forks came to rest noiselessly on the edges of plates. Dollar bills drifted onto the table. We walked out of the restaurant, back to the apartment, and directly into Jenny's bedroom in a slow-motion, soft-focus daze. We started to undress singly, then turned to undress each other, shyly at first. We were both comfortable undressing our male lovers, and we were both comfortable with each other. But to undress your best friend as you did a lover was very new. Didn't seduction depend at least in part on unfamiliarity?

We rolled onto the waterbed, and I thrilled to the feel, the smell and touch of Jenny. Softness, tenderness, and such overwhelming passion. I was half dizzy. We rubbed, we rolled, we laughed, and finally, we shared wondrous tears. Jenny claimed that now she understood why men were so hooked on women's breasts. I suddenly understood that my entire life had changed.

Jenny and I were lovers. All sorts of emotions erupted in me. I, who had been so blasé about my boyfriends, became fiercely jealous of anyone who paid attention to Jenny. When she performed and I saw a man leer appreciatively at her from the audience, I had the urge to turn the table over in his lap and scream, "Back off, you creep, she's coming home with me!" Ah, yes. Cool, intellectual Alana transformed into Anna Magnani on a rampage. In my muddled state of wonder, I gave little thought to any future, but as the week wore on, Jenny forced me to recognize some hard realities.

Being a lesbian did not appeal to her, Jenny confessed one morning as we were sipping coffee in the kitchen. It had taken her so long to believe that she was attractive to men, and she wasn't ready to throw it all away. And she didn't think she could stand to be an outcast, either. I was stunned. The word *lesbian* had not been formed yet in my own mind. We could both continue to see men, I offered. We both liked men, didn't we? Except we'd have each other as well. Jenny was evasive. Wasn't I about to move to Hawaii? Yes, but that could be changed. After all, everything seemed to have been made new in the past few days. No, Jenny felt that we should each go on with our own lives. Stunned, I had nothing else to say. It was clear that whatever the future was to be, it could not contain the two of us as lovers.

And so, when the week was out, I drove back to Chicago, sold my car, and flew to Hawaii to meet my friends. Slowly, I accepted the fact that while Jenny loved me, she was not a lesbian, and her life was going to evolve separately from mine. This affair with Jenny put me in touch with my feelings for women. For years, I seesawed between men and women before realizing that while it is easy to get in and out of bed with either sex, what is deepest in me is touched only by another woman.

Sometimes I don't see Jenny for years, but every few months we exchange a long letter or half-hour phone call. She sends me photos of her husband's paintings and of their children — blond and tall as Hitler Youth, she has commented dryly. I send her manuscripts and pictures of me with my lover and our animals. I watch her on television; she reads my work. We still care.

We never mention the week fifteen years ago when we were lovers. I don't even know if her husband knows about our affair, but I suspect that he'd think it was fine. I wonder, sometimes, if Jenny thinks about our interlude at all, and if so, how she remembers it. I know that, at that time, being a lesbian touched a place of fear in Jenny. I wonder if now that she is secure in herself, she'd remember it as a time of "rounding out" her sexual education, as an expression of love for a friend, or as the satisfaction of a curiosity.

Maybe the next time Jenny and I are both on the same coast at the same time I'll ask her how she feels about it. And then again, maybe I won't. Her response could not alter in me the bright, bittersweet memory or the quiet joy that continues to come from loving Jenny.

Emma Joy Crone

Crone Story

For me, coming out has been a continuous, growing, empowering experience – not something I can intellectualize, but a political, philosophical, and emotional way of life.

Nineteen sixty-eight found me in San Francisco, long before it became the city of freedom for homosexuals that it is today. I was newly divorced after twelve years of marriage, newly immigrating, looking for a new husband, and not at all interested in the feminist movement which was in full swing around me. I was resisting the suggestions by my friend Louise that I "go to a women's meeting." I did not want to be one of those women wearing blue jeans; I was forty years old and thought I was pretty set in the way of life that I had known all those years. However, I had always been a political being, and the fact that the invasion of Cambodia was happening and much was developing around this issue in the U.S. at that time prompted me to go with others from my place of work to a workshop in Berkeley entitled Women and Work. At this workshop, a feminist (unrecognizable as such to me because of my preconceptions) talked of what was happening on campus around women's issues. Doors flew open in my head, and on returning to my place of work, I announced to my friend Louise that I was interested in going to a consciousness-raising group. One visit, and I knew that I had always been a feminist — little did I realize that this was to be my first step to coming out.

My life up to this time had been spent in an industrial city in England. I had never heard the word *lesbian,* but when I was a young woman, someone had pointed a pub out to me where "those women" went. When I asked what this meant, my friend said, "If you go in there and sit down, they will come and talk to you and touch you on the leg" — this was my basic introduction to lesbianism. I didn't hear the word until I became involved in women's issues. Never before had I been exposed to any of the depressing, sad, inhibitory, homophobic stories I have heard since then. Sex when I was growing up meant babies, nothing more. As with many people of my generation, the joys of sensuality or sexuality with either sex were never made known to me, let alone the fact that I could enjoy my life as a woman loving women in a way totally unimagined to me.

On looking back now, it feels to me that my immigration to the U.S. at the age of forty was the real beginning of my life. My first three months were spent in the city of New York. What an experience! My life as a heterosexual in a repressive culture of working-class attitudes toward life and marriage had left me totally unprepared for the attitudes and openness I found working as a floating secretary in one of the largest cancer research establishments. The first office I worked in was with a gay man and a woman of color who thought I was a hoot because of my English expressions, and learning the American language proved to be a constant challenge of new expressions and misuse of words, such as *rubber* for *eraser.* The other difference which to me at that time was very important was the attitude toward divorce. In England, I had literally been shunned as a divorced woman in places I worked, and I felt I had failed in this aspect, then important to me, of my life as a woman. However, in the U.S., the reaction was "Is it your third or your fourth divorce?" I was stunned, and while nowadays I have a very different outlook on this attitude toward marriage, at the time it was a very freeing experience. My background had been one where one kept the marriage vows and did not look at another man (let alone a woman), and I can only now see that my marriage was a very dull and forbidding experience in my life.

I stayed in New York for three months; on hearing of the awful winters they experienced there, I decided to take a plane to sunny California. Incidentally, I should say at this point that during the whole of this adventure, I knew no one in the United States. I had taken off from England in a very sad, depressed state, convinced that my life was over and that I would just find another husband and, hey, presto, all would be well.

San Francisco at first was not too exciting: jobs were hard to find, and agencies were charging large fees to put one in touch with an employer. I lived in a Catholic hostel for women, this being the cheapest place to find that provided huge breakfasts, part of which I would take to work with me for lunch! I finally found work in a large teaching hospital, and it was there that I met Louise. We worked in the same department, had coffee breaks and lunch together, and spent many weekends at either her home or mine. Everyone was talking about us, waiting for "it" to happen.

Once I had discovered myself as a feminist, I then became involved in many sharing womanly projects that were happening around me. It was a time of great excitement and opening up for me, as for many other women at this time: skills taught

by women, art, meetings, self-defense classes, and my empow-
erment around the issue of rape. Women were opening their
homes to do projects in. I met many wonderful women, but
my awareness that I was mixing with lesbians did not come till
much later. Louise and I used to go to gay bars, as well as hang
around with lots of women. In those days there was no
Amelia's or Mama Bear's or coffeehouses for women. We just
sat watching at the women's dances we went to, never dancing
together, until one night when we finally decided to try it out.
I must mention at this time that, though feminist and involved
with all these woman-oriented happenings, we were still relating to, and sleeping with, men. I cannot believe nowadays that
I can have been so naive as to not realize that many of the
women with whom we related were lesbians. No one ever tried
to initiate us into lesbianism – contrary to societal belief about
homosexuality.

One day Louise and I were out driving, and right out of the
blue, I said to her, "Have you ever wondered what it would
be like to make love with a woman?" She gripped the steering
wheel hard.

"I don't know" was all she answered, with no more
discussion.

She was extremely quiet for the rest of the day, and I felt I
had made a faux pas and did not pursue the subject. I had no
idea where my question was coming from. We'd neither of us
during our growing-up time had the freedom to express our
needs, sexual or otherwise. So discussions around sexuality
were still taboo, and as I've said before, relating in a sexual way
to women was something neither of us had heard of. Louise,
who was also forty, had been brought up Roman Catholic, and
my upbringing, though not religious, had been completely
devoid of any knowledge about sexuality.

One weekend when I was home in bed on a Saturday night, there was a knock on the door. Louise and our gay male friend had just been to Kelly's Bar (this was in San Francisco, forty-five miles away — I was living in Sonoma County), and had decided to drop in and see me. We talked awhile (it was midnight), and then a discussion as to where to sleep ensued. The gay man decided on a piece of foam on the floor, and Louise to jump into bed with me. We were neither of us prepared for what happened, for that night I caressed a woman for the first time in my life. We didn't make love in the sense of genital sex, but we realized we were women loving each other. The next morning I was overwhelmed with delight, for not only could I be close with women as a feminist, but I could actually be lovers with women. I wanted to shout from the housetops; it was the most wonderful, amazing thing that had ever happened to me.

I was so elated with this new aspect of my life that on going to work the following Monday, I rushed into a department where I knew a young lesbian technician, and I burst out with my news. Then came my first introduction to homophobia. "Hush," she said. "You mustn't tell everyone, people don't like us." Back then I could not understand why; since then, I have learned much about society's attitudes. To this day, I am not ashamed. I have no sense that there is anything wrong in my being a lesbian; it feels the most natural way of life to me. If people don't like who I am, they don't have to relate to me. There are many wonderful lesbians in the world, so I don't feel the loneliness that many lesbians in the past have had the misfortune to experience.

I have met many lesbians while traveling in Europe and living on women's land in the United States, Denmark, England, and Canada, where I now live.

One of my greatest coming-out experiences was in Oregon, where in 1977 I went to a Gathering of Older Women (I was forty-nine at the time) happening in Wolf Creek. I went to find my peers, and there discovered myself as a writer, a spiritual woman, and, most exciting of all, a countrywoman. I had never thought I could once again find a new lifestyle and one that was more conducive to my way of living and happiness than I had yet experienced. I learned many new skills (once again from women); I learned that I did not have to have bulging muscles to chop wood, and that I had peer-counseling skills. Other women showed me how I hid my fears, and how to be a real person in my relationships with women. I felt safe to explore myself as a human being, letting go once again of many misconceptions about myself. Many workshops and many months later, I returned to Canada filled with a sense of selfhood. In Oregon, I formed nonsexual relationships with many new women who have since become my "family," but I call them my tribe. These lesbians now live in many parts of the world, and I have a tribal family with whom I keep in constant contact. It sure beats the life experience I had before the age of forty.

Country living has become for me the life I want to live for as long as I am on this planet. I see this as coming from my childhood, for when I was growing up in a smoggy, polluted city, I used to escape to the countryside, youth hosteling every weekend. The youths I was with, on looking back, were always women. I see that my life has constantly been woman-oriented, and though I never thought about it until writing this, I, like many others, went through the "crushes" on two of my schoolteachers — one the gym mistress (as they were then known) and the other my English teacher, who, I remember, had beautiful red hair and was called Miss Frost (sigh). Country life has meant that I have time to develop my skills without city distractions. I am busier than I have ever been. While always being open to challenge and learning more about myself and the world around me, I feel this is the reason that lesbianism is not hard for me. I love life, and at sixty years old, which I am now, I feel I am entering new phases, new beginnings. I recently had my first article published, I am working on watercolors, and I am taking drawing lessons. For the past four years, I have been putting out a newsletter aimed at increasing the visibility of older lesbians, hoping that this would encourage others to share their life experiences, dreams, and visions of alternatives for their future as elders to those presented by current society.

I live on one of the Gulf Islands of British Columbia, and while this can be isolating, I fill my time adequately. I have now been celibate for three years, by choice. This is not because I no longer want to love and be with women, but because I am going through a healing process — for with awareness comes the understanding of what I have been doing with most of my life, some of which has of course been quite hard to cope with. In particular, I think of menopause, that other time when I discovered my fears around aging. I found myself once again alone in that many of the women around me were younger or had had hysterectomies, and the whole of literature I discovered was written by male doctors who considered this episode in a woman's life as an affliction best ignored or doused with tranquilizers. Now there are many books written by and for women on this very different change in our lives. At that time, I took myself off to a cabin in the country where I lived alone, grew a garden, and had my hot flashes and pseudoarthritic pains and depressions. Gradually, over a period of years, I adjusted (once again) to yet another process of change in my life.

Self-discovery and personal growth work have been my constant companions, with lots of therapy with wonderful spiritual feminist lesbian workers thrown in. I use the word *workers,* rather than *counselors,* because it is all work! This continues where I live now, where I am involved with another women's group — adult children of dysfunctional families (but that is another story).

I am now meeting, through my newsletter and output to various magazines and my writing, some older lesbians. Many have grown up with the knowledge of their lesbianism, and some have worked as professionals or in jobs that have not enabled them to be "out" in the world; this can make for a lot of fear about coming out. There are others, who, while recognizing their love for women, are trapped in the so-called security of marriage. However, to all these women who may be afraid of the label of lesbianism and the connotations that society has placed on this word, I would like to say that there is joy and strength to be gained in the knowledge of oneself. As we age, why not be as we are meant to be, instead of a reflection of what others desire?

One woman I heard of through SAGE (Senior Action in a Gay Environment coming out of New York) lived alone and was referred to this organization by a social worker after having been in the closet all her life and with a partner. She said, "If I can't come out at the age of ninety-two, when can I?"

The more of us that reveal ourselves, the more society will have to accept our presence. We are a living force to be reckoned with.

SO, CRONES, COME OUT, COME OUT, WHEREVER YOU ARE!

Jewelle Gomez

I Lost It at the Movies

My grandmother, Lydia, and my mother, Dolores, were both talking to me from their bathroom stalls in the Times Square movie theatre. I was washing butter from my hands at the sink and didn't think it at all odd. The people in my family are always talking; conversation is a life force in our existence. My great-grandmother, Grace, would narrate her life story from 7 a.m. until we went to bed at night. The only break was when we were reading or the reverential periods when we sat looking out of our tenement windows, observing the neighborhood, which we naturally talked about later.

So it was not odd that Lydia and Dolores talked nonstop from their stalls, oblivious to everyone except us. I hadn't expected it to happen there, though. I hadn't really expected an "it" to happen at all. To be a lesbian was part of who I was, like being left-handed — even when I'd slept with men. When my great-grandmother asked me in the last days of her life if I would be marrying my college boyfriend I said yes, knowing I would not, knowing I was a lesbian.

It seemed a fact that needed no expression. Even my first encounter with the word *bulldagger* was not charged with emotional conflict. When I was a teen in the 1960s, my grandmother told a story about a particular building in our Boston neighborhood that had gone to seed. She described the building's past through the experience of a party she'd attended there thirty years before. The best part of the evening had been a woman she'd met and danced with. Lydia had been a professional dancer and singer on the black theater circuit; to dance with women was who she was. They'd danced, then the woman walked her home and asked her out. I heard the delicacy my grandmother searched for even in her retelling of how she'd explained to the "bulldagger," as she called her, that she liked her fine but she was more interested in men. I was struck with how careful my grandmother had been to make it clear to that woman (and, in effect, to me) that there was no offense taken in her attentions, that she just didn't "go that way," as they used to say. I was so happy at thirteen to have a word for what I knew myself to be. The word was mysterious and curious, as if from a new language that used some other alphabet which left nothing to cling to when touching its curves and crevices. But still a word existed, and my grandmother was not flinching in using it. In fact, she'd smiled at the good heart and good looks of the bulldagger who'd liked her.

Once I had the knowledge of a word and a sense of its importance to me, I didn't feel the need to explain, confess, or define my identity as a lesbian. The process of reclaiming my ethnic identity in this country was already all-consuming. Later, of course, in moments of glorious self-righteousness, I did make declarations. But they were not usually ones I had to make. Mostly, they were a testing of the waters. A preparation for the rest of the world, which, unlike my grandmother, might not have a grounding in what true love is about. My first lover, the woman who'd been in my bed once a week most of our high school years, finally married. I told her with my poems that I was a lesbian. She was not afraid to ask if what she'd read was about her, about my love for her. So there, amidst her growing children, errant husband, and bowling trophies I said yes, the poems were about her and my love for her, a love I'd always regret relinquishing to her reflexive obeisance to tradition. She did not flinch either. We still get drunk together when I go home to Boston.

During the 1970s, I focused less on career than on how to eat and be creative at the same time. Graduate school and a string of nontraditional jobs (stage manager, midtown messenger, etc.) left me so busy I had no time to think about my identity. It was a long time before I made the connection between my desire, my isolation, and the difficulty I had with my writing. I thought of myself as a lesbian between girlfriends — except the between had lasted five years. After some anxiety and frustration I deliberately set about meeting women. Actually, I knew many women, including my closest friend at the time, another black woman also in the theatre. She became uncharacteristically obtuse when I tried to open up and explain my frustration at going to the many parties we attended and being too afraid to approach women I was attracted to, certain I would be rejected because the women were either straight and horrified or gay and terrified of being exposed. For my friend, theoretical homosexuality was acceptable, even trendy. Any uncomfortable experience was irrelevant to her. She was impatient and unsympathetic. I drifted away from her in pursuit of the women's community, a phrase that was not in my vocabulary yet, but I knew it was something more than just "women." I fell into that community by connecting with other women writers, and that helped me to focus on my writing and on my social life as a lesbian.

Still, none of my experiences demanded that I bare my soul. I remained honest but not explicit. *Expediency, diplomacy, discretion* are all words that come to mind now. At that time, I knew no political framework though which to filter my experience. I was more preoccupied with the Attica riots than with Stonewall. The media helped to focus our attentions within a proscribed spectrum and obscure the connections between the issues. I worried about who would shelter Angela Davis, but the concept of sexual politics was remote and theoretical.

I'm not certain exactly when and where the theory and reality converged.

Being a black woman and a lesbian unexpectedly blended, like that famous scene in Ingmar Bergman's film *Persona*. The different faces came together as one, and my desire became part of my heritage, my skin, my perspective, my politics, and my future. And I felt sure that it had been my past that helped make the future possible. The women in my family had acted as if their lives were meaningful. Their lives were art. To be a lesbian among them was to be an artist. Perhaps the convergence came when I saw the faces of my great-grandmother, grandmother, and mother in those of the community of women I finally connected with. There was the same adventurous glint in their eyes; the same determined step; the penchant for breaking into song and for not waiting for anyone to take care of them.

I need not pretend to be other than who I was with any of these women. But did I need to declare it? During the holidays, when I brought home best friends or lovers, my family always welcomed us warmly, clasping us to their magnificent bosoms. Yet there was always an element of silence in our neighborhood, and, surprisingly enough, in our family, that was disturbing to me. Among the regulars in my father, Duke's, bar, was Maurice. He was eccentric, flamboyant, and still ordinary. He was accorded the same respect by neighborhood children as every other adult. His indiscretions took their place comfortably among the cyclical, Saturday night, man-woman scandals of our neighborhood. I regret never having asked my father how Maurice and he had become friends.

Soon, I felt the discomforting silence pressing against my life more persistently. During visits home to Boston, it no longer sufficed that Lydia and Dolores were loving and kind to the "friend" I brought home. Maybe it was just my getting older. Living in New York City at the age of thirty in 1980, there was little I kept deliberately hidden from anyone. The genteel silence that hovered around me when I entered our home was palpable, but I was unsure whether it was already there when I arrived or if I carried it home within myself. It cut me off from what I knew was a kind of fulfillment available only from my family. The lifeline from Grace, to Lydia, to Dolores, to Jewelle was a strong one. We were bound by so many things, not the least of which was looking so much alike. I was not willing to be orphaned by silence.

If the idea of cathedral weddings and station wagons held no appeal for me, the concept of an extended family was certainly important. But my efforts were stunted by our inability to talk about the life I was creating for myself, for all of us. It felt all the more foolish because I thought I knew how my family would react. I was confident they would respond with their customary aplomb, just as they had when I'd first had my hair cut as an Afro (which they hated) or when I brought home friends who were vegetarians (which they found curious). While we had disagreed over some issues, like the fight my mother and I had over Vietnam when I was nineteen, always when the deal went down, we sided with each other. I think, somewhere deep inside, I believed that neither my grand-mother nor my mother would ever censure my choices. Neither had actually raised me; my great-grandmother had done that, and she had been a steely barricade against any encroachment on our personal freedoms, and she'd never disapproved out loud of anything I'd done.

But it was not enough to have an unabashed admiration for these women. It is one thing to have pride in how they'd so graciously survived in spite of the odds against them. It was something else to be standing in a Times Square movie theater faced with the chance to say "it" out loud and risk the loss of their brilliant and benevolent smiles.

My mother had started reading the graffiti written on the wall of the bathroom stall. We hooted at each of her dramatic renderings. Then she said (not breaking her rhythm, since we all know timing is everything), "Here's one I haven't seen before: 'DYKES UNITE.'" There was that profound silence again, as if the frames of my life had ground to a halt. We were in a freeze-frame, and options played themselves out in my head in rapid succession: Say nothing? Say something? Say what?

I laughed and said, "Yeah, but have you seen the rubber stamp on my desk at home?"

"No," said my mother with a slight bit of puzzlement. "What does it say?"

"I saw it," my grandmother called out from her stall. "It says: 'Lesbian Money!'"

"What?"

"'Lesbian Money,'" Lydia repeated.

"I just stamp it on my big bills," I said tentatively, and we all screamed with laughter. The other woman at the sinks tried to pretend we didn't exist.

Since then there has been little discussion. There have been some moments of awkwardness, usually in social situations where they feel uncertain. Although we have not explored the "it," the shift in our relationship is clear. When I go home, it is with my lover, and she is received as such. I was lucky. My family was as relieved as I to finally know who I was.

Susan J. Friedman

Notes for a Coming-Out Story

I.

Write about why it's important. Why it's still important. Why all of our stories are important, because mine is different from hers is different from yours. Because I came out in 1980, three months before Reagan was elected, and you came out in 1960, nine years before Stonewall, and the year I was born. Because she came out in 1973, at the height of feminism's "second wave." Because someone killed herself because of it. And because someone got married and raised three children before she knew she was a lesbian, and lost them all, every last one, in a custody battle. Because someone went to her senior prom in 1990 with her girlfriend and the next day "DYKE LEZZIE QUEER" was painted all over her front walk. Because we are becoming braver and more numerous. Because we have always been brave and numerous. Because I grew up a Jew, and in the Jewish tradition, stories are to be told again and again and again, each year a cycle of the telling, of the retelling. Because the coming-out story will not be obsolete until all hatred of queerness is obsolete. May this happen speedily and in my day and generation, amen.

II.

I am six years old. In the first grade at Superior Elementary School. My principal is Miss Conklin. My teacher is Mrs. Kregenow. Some kids call her "Mrs. Kangaroo," but not me; I never do that. I love Mrs. Kregenow. I also love Heather. Heather is beautiful. She is in my class. She is friends with Jeanetta. Heather and Jeanetta both wear pretty dresses, but Heather's are prettier. My favorite is black, with little green flowers and white puffy sleeves. Heather has long, blonde hair and white white skin, and she looks like a flower when she runs. I'm going to ask Mommy to get me a dress just like hers.

III.

I am sixteen. I go to an all-girls private "alternative" school. A groovy school. We talk about abortion, debate the existence of God, and read *Zen and the Art of Motorcycle Maintenance* in English class. No one talks about lesbians. I am sixteen, and one night I have a dream. I dream that my friend Kitty kisses me. Right on the lips. Smack. Smack on the lips, wet and juicy. No mistaking what *that* means. And I write in my diary, my tiny, brown diary that I keep hidden in the deep recesses of my bedroom: "I had a dream that Kitty K. kissed me right on the lips, and it sickened me, so that must prove *something*, but how ashamed I felt after that dream ... What if I could turn out to be a homosexual or something?!"

IV.

Nineteen years old, away at college. Nineteen years old, away at college, and lusting after Kate, the drama queen next door. Only, I don't call it lust. If I called it anything, the word would be *love*. Or *crush*. Possibly *infatuation*. My best friends, Amy and Emily, have infatuations all the time. We call them "dithers." Amy, particularly, is always in a "dither" over some boy. Sometimes, on a Saturday night, we go out to the one movie showing in Gambier, Ohio — Emily and some boy, Amy and some boy, and me. Or we go to a frat party, where I stand in a corner, nursing one beer that lasts all night. We talk about everything, the three of us: alienation in modern industrial society, Anaïs Nin, feminism, chamber music, marijuana, our families. We talk about everything except one thing. One thing: the electricity that darts and zigs and zags whenever I am in a room with Kate. We don't talk about it and we don't talk about it and we don't talk about it, until, finally, something inside me burns to a fine crisp.

V.

"Gay and Lesbian Hotline..."
    Silence.
    "This is the Gay and Lesbian Hotline. Can I help you?"
    Click.

In the library, the same library I've been biking to since I was ten, I look it up. I look it up all ways. *Lesbian. Gay. Homosexual.* I find *Rubyfruit Jungle*. I cannot take it out. I cannot put it down. I sit in a study carrel at the Mayfield Library in Mayfield Heights, Ohio, for three hours, reading. When I put the book down, I am sure. I am sure I am a lesbian. I am twenty years old.

VI.

I am twenty-three. "Why did you have to tell your grand-mother on Chanukah?!"

VII.

Harvard Square on a hot June night. Sweat drips down my neck in rivulets, as I stand, staring blankly at magazines on display at the Out-of-Town newsstand. Suddenly, a headline catches my eye. And a picture. Two women, holding each other, on the cover of *Newsweek*? I stare, and stare some more. I take out my wallet and buy the magazine. As I am handing bills to the boy at the register, it flashes through my mind: "Uh-oh, will he think...?" I sit down on a warm cement slab to read the article. Again, thoughts flash: "What if someone sees me?" Sees me — me and that word, writ way too large and bold across the cover: *Lesbians*. And suddenly I think it is like the word *Jew* and how I sometimes talk too loud and move my hands too much, and it is like the yellow stars my father and my uncle had to wear, in the camps, beside men who wore pink triangles, and suddenly, goddamnit, I am a *lesbian*, I am who I am. And I unfold the magazine.

I am thirty-three years old.

Gillian Hanscombe

Sweating, Thumping, Telling

I'm sitting at a double desk (replete with two removable, white porcelain inkwells being filled from a large bottle by the ink monitor) second to the back row, in an Australian state school classroom. It's 1952, and I'm seven years old. Diagonally behind me sits Glenys Hill, who taps me on the shoulder, wanting to borrow a pencil. I turn around. With what I later learn from books is a thumping heart, I think in words, "I love Glenys Hill!"

Then I'm nine, walking round the back of the girls' shelter-shed, where we eat packed lunches, arm in arm with Terrie Fisher. I say to her, "I love you." She says, "Do you mean like a man loves a woman?" Oh yes, I'm about to say, oh yes. But she goes on, "Or like a friend loves a friend?" I say "yes" to that, knowing nothing, but somehow knowing this second yes is the correct yes.

Next I'm twelve. I've gone to a fee-paying girls' school run by Church of England nuns, where my mother had been a boarder thirty years before. I'm entranced by a bigger girl deigning to talk to me. She's called Maxine and is frightfully strong. She's fourteen and hits tennis balls harder than anyone in the school. She teaches me to hit tennis balls too, every morning before school (I get up at seven to be there for as long as possible) and every afternoon (my mother rages when I'm not home until eight at night). Our fingers touch as we sway about standing squashed together in the athletics team bus. I sweat and thump like anything. She writes me hugely long letters, hugely long poems in the style of Tennyson, Milton, and the Shakespeare of the History plays, though I won't know the originals until much later. We "wrestle" in the cloakrooms. She calls it wrestling and she always wins, but I don't mind a bit being pinned down by her. "I love you," she says fiercely against my sweating ear, my burning head held hard down flat on the concrete. The other girls snigger when they catch us, but I'm only dimly aware that they don't do these things.

It's the holidays. I spend a week at Maxine's house. Both her parents go to work, so we're alone. We spend all day in bed, hugging and kissing, declaring passion, kissing some more. We don't take our clothes off and don't know what else to do, other than kissing and hugging.

After a year, my mother confronts me. She's found my shoeboxes stuffed with Maxine's letters and poems. She burns them all. She's worried about me. On the advice of the family doctor, a woman, my mother makes me join a mixed church fellowship and a mixed dancing class. I get crushes on the young woman who runs the church fellowship and on one of the girls at the dancing class, but I don't tell anyone. I kiss all the boys who want to kiss me, but my heart never thumps. I only care that one or other of them kisses me, so I can pass with the other girls.

I fall in love with God for a while, and then with my English teacher, who's twenty-two. I'm fifteen, and she spends time with me out of school, telling me about modern poetry and herself. We hug and kiss a lot, but she won't let me take her clothes off. I vaguely want to, though. My father thinks this friendship is "unhealthy" and gets my mother to send me to see the doctor again. The doctor prescribes more "mixed" activities and activity generally.

Then I'm sixteen and in my last year of school. My heart thumps again. She's called Patsie and is a boarder at a different school. We've met on and off for years when our schools have played each other at tennis, softball, basketball, and so on. We make friends and write letters. She spends a boarders' weekend with me. I stay at her house over the holidays, and we lie in bed together, declaring love and passion. One night she says, "I don't think either of us has any inhibitions," and slips her hand down my pajama waist, down my belly, down to my pubic hair. I do the same to her. I wonder what all the sticky wet is, having no idea. We rub a lot...

Her mother phones my mother. She's opened a letter I posted to Patsie. She says to my mother, "I've never *seen* such a letter in my life. I would never write such a letter to my own husband." "And she has five children," my mother explains to me, dreadfully distressed. I can't make it out. My letter has words in it like *breasts* and *hair* and *thighs*. Wanting them, that is. Wanting Patsie. Don't wives want their husbands, then? Patsie's mother doesn't seem to. My mother doesn't seem to, either. Women don't??

I'm sent to another doctor. She says it will all pass. She says I should meet more boys. I've already met all the boys the other girls have met. "Meet more then," she says heartily.

Later, I'm sent for psychoanalysis. I do that for four years, and it makes me better and stronger and saner. During that time, I have Kerryn and Ruth and Kate and others ... By now, I know the word *lesbian* (it's in the books) and the word *orgasm* (it's in the same books), and I've had sex with men, but it never once made my heart thump.

I'm twenty-three and living with a lover called D. We plan to go to Europe and live in England for a bit. She's a musician. I want to travel and write, but what I really want to do is get away with being a lesbian. A couple of years later, on a visit back home, I talk to my mother. She worries all the time about me being "alone" and "not settled" in England. "I'm not alone," I tell her. "If you're going to worry, it may as well be about something true rather than something not true. D is my lover. We live together and sleep together. I'm a lesbian. I'm not alone."

My mother mourns. She's a Christian and thinks it's wrong and that she's wrong and what did she do wrong? "Nothing," I tell her, but it's no use. She mourns and worries and blames herself. But she doesn't change toward me.

Three years later, my mother dies suddenly. I plan to have a baby and become pregnant. I lose that baby and try again, this time successfully. I learn about feminism and gay liberation. I join things, start writing differently, and feel better and better about being lesbian. But I'm not too sure I can pinpoint my coming out. If you live like a lesbian before you know the word, it all just feels like going on and growing up.

Linda Heal

Life after Pantyhose

Only a week before, we had done our first loads of laundry together at college. Carefully following my mom's written instructions, we separated the whites and colors, and then, at fifty cents per load, decided to consolidate everything into one machine — we'd deal with laundry that didn't win awards.

We were eighteen and freshmen at a small liberal arts college in an Illinois town of about 100,000. It was September of 1983, and the first class I went to was Social Problems, where I sat behind a quietly intense woman in beat-up running shoes. Being an ex-jock, I'm always looking at the quality of people's footwear to see how seriously they take themselves. That person turned out to be Kay, and on an October evening, we decided to get together to study for our college exam premiere in Social Problems.

We opted to study while walking on Main Street — Kay was constantly in motion, so this studying on foot wasn't uncharacteristic. We had barely touched the material in Section One when she sat down in a flower box in front of a tanning spa and perched on its edge.

"Can I trust you?" she said. "And can you trust me?" I nodded to both of these and I heard in the rhythm of Kay's voice that if the pacing of her questions slowed, she would never get her words out. "Are you gay or straight? Me, I'm as queer as a three-dollar bill."

And there it was in a chill over Main Street – the question I'd avoided thinking about for the past five years. But there was something new, a good reason to say, "Yeah. Maybe," to a supportive person asking it. So I said it. "Yeah, maybe. I mean, I've always thought I probably was, but I've never had the opportunity. I've never checked it out." And I hadn't. I grew up in a midwestern town of 14,000 that acted even smaller. Openly gay men and women were as hard to find as tasteful radio stations, so I was stuck without role models, or even accepting people to talk with about what I thought was happening with me. Once when I was fourteen and tried to bring it up with Mom, all I could say was, "Mom, the other kids are calling me gay." I choked on what I wanted to say next: "And I think they're right."

I first realized there was such a thing as homosexuality when I was eleven and watching the previews for the next week's episode of *Family*. One of Willie's friends had come out to him, and then they cut to the preview scene where mother Kate talks to daughter Buddy – "Do you know what a homosexual is, Buddy?"

"Yeah. A guy who likes a guy or a girl who likes a girl."

The preview didn't open any doors for me – in fact, by the next week when the actual episode was on, I had to ask at the first commercial break what homosexuality was. But after that, I remembered.

I had just turned thirteen when I noticed my attachments to my new female friends seemed somehow different, kind of romantic. I hesitantly admitted it a year later in my journal, about fifteen pages after I talked about how close I felt to

Michelle and Julie, how much I respected them because they ignored the other kids who kept asking me if I was going to have a husband or a wife, or if Renee Richards was my hero. I knew that my love surpassed ordinary love and respect — I just knew that nobody felt as passionate about members of their own gender as I felt about Julie and Michelle.

"I think I'm gay," I wrote in my early teen handwriting that vacillated between the large loopy way everybody else wrote and my own tight pointy letters. "It isn't from other people calling me that — I just have what adults would call 'very confusing feelings.' Damn right, they're confusing. I'm not attracted to boys at all. I want to be with Julie and I want to do with her the things I'm supposed to want to do with boys. Damn it, what's going on? I think I love her. What's the matter with me?"

Clearly, I was different from the other eighth-graders, and my peers had noticed. I could live with being different, because I came with an intact sense of self-esteem. When people ask me what role my family played in my lesbianism, I tell them, "They encouraged me to feel self-esteem, even though I didn't yet know I was a lesbian, so that I could face up to who I was and wouldn't stifle myself by pretending I'm something I'm obviously not." Because of this self-esteem and a good sense of humor, I was accepted, even if I was "the weird one."

Despite my feeling comfortable much of the time in the face of being called "weird," knowing that I was a lesbian also frightened me. It frightened me so much, I went into hiding for four years. I never acted on my feelings for women, hoping that eventually they'd evolve into heterosexual feelings. I could even be spotted at high school dances, being a good sport about the death by pantyhose I was suffering underneath the long dresses I wore to those events.

All the while I knew that I was shushing a chunky part of myself, and that hurt. I stopped writing journals, because introspection was dangerous. I stopped reading, because I never knew when a teenage character would strike some nerve and I'd get upset. I poured myself into being busy — I played volleyball, basketball, softball, wrote the yearbook, and fell in love with early-American literature, which seemed safely removed, reading these stories that never talked about love, only solitary men freezing to death on tundras.

All that squelching had brought me here, to a flower box on Main Street, where I finally decided that what I had been ignoring might have some positive force.

Kay and I kept walking and talking, and I was finally able to share my confusion and the pain of hiding with someone who knew what it was all about. I could ask somebody else the questions I'd been stewing about. It was Kay, for instance, who made me realize that maybe it just doesn't matter how we got to be lesbian in the first place. "That's all history," she said. "What we need to deal with is now. We can choose to accept the fact that things work out differently for us than for most people. Or we can choose to ignore it."

I had tried ignoring it, and that was extremely uncomfortable. Now, I was one hundred miles away from my hometown, family, and all the people that would hold me to my past, and was more than ready for a clean start.

Kay told me that she found me attractive and, if I wouldn't feel too crowded, perhaps we could start seeing each other romantically. On Main Street, we started what was to be a sixteen-month relationship.

At first, there were a lot of secretive smiles — it felt like a secret affair, and the sparks I felt with Kay were something new, coming so easily and naturally after all those high school years when I had tried to convince myself that I felt there was some sort of fleshy interest in the guy I was dating. When we slept together three weeks later, lovemaking came very easily. There was an undeniable feeling in my flesh that this was how things are best for me, that I was meant to love a woman's softness.

Coming out to myself, as much as it was a relief, was still a stressful time for me. My roommate, a petite prom queen with a tiny squeaky voice, found out that Kay and I were more than friends. She freaked out and moved out — evidence that I was now a social nasty. I noticed an increasing distance when I talked with Mom; every time I picked up the phone I tried to become who I'd been in high school, and the fast transitions between the two worlds made my ears ring.

When things got tough for me, I remembered that it was even more uncomfortable denying who I was. It seemed I'd been given my choice of pains, and I chose to face the pains that would move me closer to being a strong person. Although I'd been in hiding for four years, the distress had never abated. After coming out, my dealings with other people's nonacceptance could at least be balanced with self-esteem.

As I became more and more comfortable with myself and other gay students through the gay student support group at a nearby larger university, I realized that I needed to let Mom know. We'd always had a close relationship and she was good at not meddling and at letting me try the things I needed to do. Mom's laissez-faire attitude allowed me to take a lot of responsibility and earned my respect, because she trusted me as much as she did. I thought Mom would want to know that I was in love for the first time. As insightful as Mom is, she probably already knew that I had lesbian leanings, I told myself as I headed downstairs one weekend to help her with the dishes.

To my surprise, telling her caught her completely off-balance, as though just moments before she'd been planning to talk to me about birth-control methods. She hadn't made anything of my lack of kinship with the high school guys I'd dated, and hadn't made any assumptions about my intense connections with my women friends. Either my heterosexual facade had been too convincing, or Mom, like me, had worked at ignoring many things.

Mom finally believed me when she realized I intended to live as a lesbian, and she went through a lot of blaming. First she blamed Kay, saying, "Maybe you just want the bond of her friendship so much you'll do whatever she tells you to — even act like a lover." When I reiterated that I'd had these feelings for women long before I met Kay, Mom started blaming herself. She said, "I guess Dad and I don't show enough affection for each other in front of you, and you haven't seen how strong male-female love can be."

Mom's insistence on seeing things this way put a new strain on our relationship. I felt that she was knocking my strength as a human — how *dare* she assert that I was weak enough to be made into a puppet by anyone, including Kay. Further, I felt that she was ignoring my ability to love, something she'd nurtured in me. I had trusted my mother to trust my judgment, and she'd let me down for the first time. I didn't want my relationship with Mom to get stuck at that point, but I knew that I wouldn't break things off with Kay in an attempt to fix things with Mom.

Mom and I had constant dialogue when I was home over weekends. We had to look through our hurts and make efforts to know what the other was feeling. Mom needed to see that I was the same person, that I wasn't rebelling against every value that she'd ever taught me, but taking that value scheme with me into my lesbian life. She needed to see that being a lesbian was a whole way of loving, not just a string of sexual encounters. I had to try not to be too hurt when she insinuated that perhaps this was just a phase, that I could change. And I had to consider that her sudden disorientation sometimes colored our talks differently, and I had to remember to be gentle with her when I wanted to be indignant or self-righteous. Our efforts to understand went both ways, and Mom started to accept me, while I learned to be patient, and thrilled, with her gradual progression.

The longevity of my relationship with Kay convinced Mom that I was sure about what I was doing. As my sixteen-month relationship with Kay progressed, Mom made genuine efforts to like her and began trying to get used to the idea that we were happy together.

In the two years since my relationship with Kay ended, Mom has made tremendous strides and now accepts me. This makes me the envy of my gay friends, who are all in some stage of dealing with, or not dealing with, their parents. Mom is ready to donate some positive books to our high school library, because there's nothing there about homosexuality, and there are some kids who really need to read about what they're going through. Mom has met all my favorite lesbian friends and has genuinely enjoyed the women I love.

My father, my younger brother and sister, and Mom's parents all know now, and I think it was Mom's patient acceptance that kept them from saying, "Ewww, gross," when she told them. My grandparents kept hoping for a change, but now, three years later, they make it even clearer that they love me. My brother and sister were twelve and fourteen when they found out − an age when being "different" isn't always welcome. Since that age was their own time of stumbling into sexual awareness, my lesbianism isn't something we talk about too much. But since they're sensitive and we all really enjoy each other, I think they see that gay people aren't only the lisping-queen stereotypes that show up in homophobic jokes.

Things have worked out extremely well for me, despite an understandably rough start. I feel so much more genuine for having accepted my lesbianism and having integrated that acceptance into my family relationships. All the coming-out scrapes and bruises seem a bargain to me now. I know how it feels to have my sexuality in the open, and how it feels to enjoy the acceptance of the people I love the most – including myself.

Karen X. Tulchinsky

Right Back Where I Started From

When I was a child, I thought I was going to grow up and marry a woman. I believed it with all my heart and soul. At bedtime, when my mother would read fairy tales to me and my sister, I'd imagine myself as the prince, perched handsomely on top of a majestic horse, riding from town to town, searching for my one true princess. I was the knight in shining armor who went off into the countryside to slay dragons and bring back their heads for my queen. When I played house with my best friend, Brenda, I was the father and she was the mother. I was the doctor, she was the nurse.

Brenda was my first girlfriend. We were small children when we first started playing together and as adolescence crept into our growing bodies, I began to fall in love with her. By the time I was eleven, I adored her. I loved her long, brown, wavy hair and how it bounced on her shoulders when she walked. I loved her sparkling, dark eyes and the way she'd throw back her head and laugh at all my jokes. When she began to develop hips and breasts, I admired her maturity. Although I had never given her a ring, in my mind, we were going steady. Every day, we walked to school together, ate

lunch together, and passed notes during class. Every afternoon, I carried her books home. I thought we would go on like
that forever.

One morning in 1969, during the first week of sixth grade,
my whole life changed. The teacher had asked us to write a
one-page essay on the natural habitat of the Canada goose. As
I began writing, my pencil point snapped on the page. I pushed
back my wooden chair and walked up the aisle to the front of
the class to wait in the pencil sharpener line. I was thinking
about what I would write, vaguely aware of the scraping of
pencils, pages being turned in notebooks, the click-click of my
teacher's high heels as she walked up and down the rows, and
then, the familiar touch of Brenda's elbow playfully digging
into my side as she joined me in the line. I turned around and
smiled at her. Something was going on. Her face looked
different. She was beaming as she held up her hand and
showed me a dime-store ring, sitting prominently on her
finger.

"It's from Neil," she whispered, proudly. "We're going
steady."

Her words slammed up against my heart cruelly, before
settling in my brain. I could hear them circling around in my
head, as I tried to understand their meaning. My throat
clamped shut and I swallowed hard, staring at Brenda in
disbelief. My legs felt suddenly weak, and for a minute, I
thought I was going to faint. In an instant, the ways of the
world became clear to me. Brenda was going steady with
Neil, not with me. She was a girl. He was a boy. Until that
moment, I had never questioned my childhood dream of
growing up and marrying a woman. Suddenly, everything
was backwards. If what Brenda was saying was true, then I
was supposed to go steady with boys, too. I was eleven years

old and no one had taught me about sex yet. My mind was not yet ingrained with the teachings of compulsory heterosexuality. This was my first moment of conscious indoctrination and I was frightened to the bottom of my being. Somehow, I turned away from her, sharpened my pencil, and went back to my seat, where I sat in a stupor for the rest of the morning. When the bell rang, I charged out of class without waiting for Brenda and ran home, crying all the way. I told my mother I wasn't feeling well and stayed home for the rest of the day.

That night I barely slept. My mind was spinning; emotions were tearing at me from the inside out. I was trying to comprehend what had happened that day. Life had taken an unexpected turn. Everything looked different: the bedroom I shared with my sister, the trees on my street, my own face. My belly turned over and over, adrenaline ran through my veins; voices, words raced around in my head. I drifted in and out of sleep, while dreams I did not want to have overtook me. Images I did not know were there danced in the darkened room, like clowns mocking me. A bride in a white wedding gown walked down the aisle, her face covered by a veil. A man in a black tuxedo waited for her. The images moved closer and I could see that the man's face was my face. He lifted the veil and the bride's face was mine also. The audience started yelling. "Men and women, boys and girls. Going steady. Neil and Brenda."

I woke up in a sweat, my heart pounding, my belly fluttering in fear. That night, I aged. In the morning when I woke up I could see it in my face. I could feel it in my bones. I was no longer a child, full of wonder, excitement, and innocence. I was almost a teenager, and what should have been some of the best years of my life, were weighed down by the newfound knowledge that I was not right, that I was different somehow, that what I wanted I could not have. I did not have the words for what I was feeling, but from that moment on I was troubled and I knew there was no one I could talk to about it. There was no one who would understand.

After that day, Brenda and I drifted apart. She stopped walking to school with me and started walking with Neil. From then on, *he* carried her books home instead of me. Brenda and I still saw each other, but things were never the same between us. I began to carefully watch her and the other girls around me, searching for clues on how to behave like a "real" girl. I tried to copy them as best I could and, from the age of thirteen until the age of eighteen, I played at being straight. I went out on dates with boys. I let them kiss and touch me. I did what I was supposed to do. I have no clear memories of that time: my days as a heterosexual blur together into one prolonged, uncomfortable, backseat grope. Boys' clumsy hands under my shirt; sloppy kisses; heavy bodies; wet tongues; bumbling hands, fumbling with clothes; awkward, inept advances, pushing, pushing, always pushing at me for more.

I kissed the boys out of duty, and all the while I lusted after my new best friend, Rifka. I'd sit in her room watching her put on her makeup. As she sat on her bed in nothing but her underpants and bra, I tried not to look. I tried not to think about her later, in my bed at night, when my hand would find its way inside my pajamas. No one had specifically said that my feelings about her were wrong, but somehow I knew it was something I should keep to myself.

When I was thirteen, I started going to United Synagogue Youth, a Sunday afternoon social and cultural group for Jewish teenagers. There, I met Tova. We liked each other right away and became instant friends. She was more sophisticated and intelligent than most of my other girlfriends. She knew more about sex and drugs and life than I did and I remember sometimes being in awe of her knowledge. Her mother was more lenient than mine and she would let us smoke cigarettes and pot in their house. Tova was a wild kid and together we had a lot of fun.

During that time I remember brainwashing myself.

"I'd rather have a boy than be one," I'd say, although it wasn't true. I was a baby butch and I had no words, no context, no hope of being who I was. I was James Dean in a black leather jacket, leaning up against a brick city wall, one foot up behind me, cigarette dangling from my lips, hands thrust coolly inside my pockets. I was Mick Jagger, prancing across the stage, sexy in torn jeans and a tight t-shirt, crooning my rock and roll ballads to all the beautiful girls in the front row. I knew I wasn't a boy, but I felt like one. Deep inside I wanted what they wanted.

I tried to be straight. I really did. I even went out with a boy named Bruce for two years, faithfully schlepping him home for every family wedding, bar mitzvah, and funeral. Eventually, we tried to have sex. I went on the pill and we waited until his parents were away for the weekend. Johnny Carson was on TV in the background. We undressed. We followed all the rules. Him on top. Me on the bottom. In, out. In, out. It didn't feel particularly good. I was dry and uninspired. It hurt. I was grateful when it was over. We watched the rest of Johnny Carson. Charo was on that night and I got more aroused watching her. Bruce drove me home and I sat up all night thinking.

The next day I knew what I had to do. Over dinner at a local Chinese restaurant, I broke up with him. He begged me to stay, but I had no feelings for him. I was eighteen, it was 1977, and I just couldn't fake it anymore. I gave him back his ring, kissed him on the cheek, and left him with the sweet-and-sour chicken balls. Walking out that door, I felt suddenly light and I knew what I wanted to do next, although I didn't yet know why. I wanted to see Tova. Her image flashed into my head and refused to leave. We went to different high schools, and though I still considered her my friend, we hadn't seen each other in almost two years. The last time we had talked, it was over the phone.

"What would you do," she had said, "if you found out one of your friends was doing something the rest of the world thought was wrong, but it felt really good, and it wasn't hurting anyone?"

I shrugged. "If she's not hurting anyone else, I guess it's okay," I said.

"Yeah? That's good. I mean, is that how you really feel?"

"Uh ... yeah ... well, I mean, I guess it depends on what it is, you know." I was getting the feeling she was looking for something from me, but I had no idea what it was. For three hours we stayed on the phone, going back and forth in this way, her trying to tell me something, but not really saying anything. I was growing impatient.

"So, what is it?" I pushed.

"Give me a second." She sounded angry.

"Come on, Tova. Whatever it is, it couldn't be that bad."

"Well, it's just that..." She sighed deeply. We were getting nowhere. I waited in silence. "It's just that ... well, it's not like I'm sure or anything, but I think I might be ... you know ... gay."

As she said it, sirens rang in my body and my heart sped up.

"Oh ... yeah?" I stammered. I went on to say something stupid, like "That's okay with me," or "Hey, I still like you anyway." Whatever I said, it wasn't quite right and a gulf formed between us. Even over the phone, I could feel her pull away. One minute we were standing side by side; the next, a huge crack split the earth between us as we stood helplessly watching the ground underneath moving in opposite directions until there was a deep canyon separating us. After that, Tova stopped calling me and I stopped calling her, until somehow two years went by with no contact.

I didn't know why Tova's image popped into my head the second I broke up with Bruce. I only knew that it did and I had to see her. I dialed her mother's number and found out that she had moved out on her own a few months earlier. I called her new number and she invited me to come right over. When I knocked on her door, she opened it a crack.

"Before I let you in," she announced, "I want you to know that Dini and I are lovers."

Lovers. The word excited me, made me nervous. "Yeah." I tried to sound as casual as I could. "I know."

She opened the door wider and let me come inside. The gesture was to be the most significant one of my life since the pencil sharpener incident. When Tova opened that door, it was the beginning of my journey back to myself, back to the little girl who knew she was going to grow up and marry a woman. That night, Tova and Dini took me to my first gay bar.

The Studio, in downtown Toronto, was rumored to have been run by the Mafia. During the week it was a major motion picture distribution office. On weekends, it was a gay bar. By coincidence, that first time I went, it was Halloween night. All over the three-story building were dozens of unusually tall

Barbra Streisands, Diana Rosses, and Tina Turners. I found out the following week that on a regular Saturday night there would be only a handful of drag queens, but on that first night, the place was full of them. From the moment they checked our I.D.s and we walked through the doors, I loved it. In The Studio, I was Dorothy and this was the Land of Oz. I was Alice and this was Wonderland. Although technically I was still straight, I did not feel out of place. I felt like I belonged there, among the tall queens and the tough butches; the flannel-shirted, overall-wearing, short-haired, androgynous women; and the thin disco boys in their too-tight pants. Standing against the wall, watching men dance with men, women with women, I felt as if someone had opened the blinds and I was seeing into a whole new world, but one that was familiar somehow. It was as if it had always been there, only out of focus. That night, undefined images became sharp, while long-buried feelings inside me began to stir, preparing for their journey to the surface.

I began to spend most of my free time with Tova and Dini, going to the bar, hanging out at their apartment, getting high, and talking about how we were going to change the world. Sometimes I worried that I was crowding them, but they didn't seem to mind. I didn't think about it too much, but at that point, if you had asked me, I'd have said I was still straight. One day, however, that changed. The transition must have been gradual, but I remember it as happening all at once. I was alone with Tova and when I looked into her eyes, I was aware of something different. I was feeling attracted to her, drawn to her. When she looked at me, it was with a new intensity, and her gaze made my belly flip. Her eyes were not just eyes anymore. They took on a dreamy quality and I could almost jump inside and drown in them.

Every time I was around Tova after that night, I had trouble breathing, I was restless, my senses were heightened. When she accidentally brushed against me, my body reacted. I wanted her to touch me and would make up excuses for her to do so, like asking her to pass the salt or the ketchup. I knew that I was in love with her, but how could it be? Wasn't I straight? Wasn't Tova in love with Dini? How could I be in love with this friend I had known so long? How could I be in love with someone who already had a lover? How could I break up their home? I was disgusted with myself and was sure these feelings were my own. I had no idea until much later that Tova was attracted to me, too.

For the next few weeks, I stayed away from her. I was scared of my strange new feelings, and I ran from them. I was so removed from myself after years of playing straight that I made no connection with my long-lost childhood dreams. And yet, the whole time I stayed away, I thought of no one but her. When she finally called to ask where I'd been and to invite me over, the sound of her voice penetrated deep into my heart and I knew I could never say no to her. I knew that whatever was going to happen between us could not be stopped. Deep in my soul I knew it was my destiny. False ethics and learned behavior were trying to rule my life, but in the end, the force of my body would win out. The little baby butch who dreamed of finding a princess of her own was back on her horse. The hinges on the drawbridge that had been sealed shut all those years ago in the pencil sharpener line were beginning to loosen. If I had listened closely, I could have heard them squeak.

I put down the phone, slipped into a pair of baggy green army pants, pulled on my work boots and my best flannel shirt, and caught a bus to her place. When I arrived, I was surprised to find her alone. It was two days before Christmas and Dini had gone to spend time with her mother. I went inside and sat down on the couch with Tova. We were both extremely nervous. Sexual energy was flowing freely throughout the apartment. Whenever I'd look into her eyes, a warm feeling started in my belly and spread throughout my body. Cloud nine could not even begin to describe how happy I felt just to be with her. I imagined taking her in my arms and kissing her, but I wasn't sure how to get there. For hours we talked, dancing around the issue, looking meaningfully into each other's eyes, but not saying anything about it. Finally, by accident, our fingers touched. We grabbed hands and held on. In slow motion, without a word, we moved toward each other. I saw her lips moving closer to mine. It seemed to take forever and then we were kissing. Her kiss was softer than I'd ever imagined. I pulled her down onto me and I plunged through a time zone. Her body against mine brought back old memories, forgotten dreams. I was home. I was right back where I'd started from. I was me again. I was a prince and she was my princess. I was a knight in shining armor and she was my queen. We kissed for hours and then slowly undressed each other. My body delighted in her touch. After years spent playing at being straight, faking it with boys, I had no idea that sex could feel so good. All night long we made love, and as we did, I crossed a line. I traversed centuries and I knew I would never be the same again: baby butch returns in all her glory. Someone had turned on the light at the end of the tunnel and I could finally see my way clear.

Somewhere in the back of my mind I knew that what we were doing was not honorable. Tova was cheating on Dini and I was colluding. We were young and reckless, and our actions had no consequences then. When you're that age, you live in the moment, and that moment was all body and no mind. The moment was passion and lust and we couldn't have stopped it if we had tried. I could have died then and it would have been the happiest day of my life. I had grown up, and even if I hadn't actually married a woman, I was, at least, kissing one.

Sarah Holmes

Groundworks

Even before I came out, I often felt I was a lesbian. I resolved that question when I was twenty-six, living in Boston and active in the feminist movement. In the twelve years since then, I have kept discovering new facets of being lesbian. It seems as though coming out is something that never ends; it evolves. Although there was an intense moment of recognition, when I said, "Yes, this is who I am," coming out is about continually uncovering and affirming feelings for and connections with women. I come out every time I hold an open conversation about my life in a public place, read a lesbian book or newspaper on the subway, or speak publicly on a lesbian issue. Although now I'm out to almost everybody in my life, there are always situations where I question whether to explain who I am or "pass."

Growing up having close and physical relationships with girls made me feel different. When I was a child, I told my mother repeatedly that I was never going to get married, and I was very stubborn about it. I was never able to envision myself in that kind of a relationship with a man; the idea of being married always seemed alien.

I explored sex before most kids in my neighborhood did, and I had a very sexual relationship with a girlfriend of mine that started when I was seven and continued for many years. We lived in a midwestern city, and would spend Saturday nights sleeping over at each other's houses before being delivered back to our respective families the next Sunday morning at church. We were eager to go to bed, seldom arguing to stay up late to watch TV. We would go into the bedroom and stay up all night playing in bed, with candles or a low light burning. Once we were caught when I put my pink bathrobe over the lamp to create a warm erotic glow and the lamp caught the robe on fire.

That quelled things for a while, because we were worried that our parents would wonder what two nine-year-old girls were doing in the middle of the night with no pajamas on.

We played witches, taking turns being good and bad, making each other do pleasurable and "naughty" things to each other. We traveled over each other's bodies, and through each other's minds and fantasies this way for years, and when we didn't see each other as much because I moved to Madison, Wisconsin, I came away knowing that it was possible to have that kind of physical intimacy with another girl. I found out from a baby-sitter what grownups did to make babies. She said that they got on top of one another and rubbed their private parts together. That was what Jane and I did, and it didn't make sense to me that I had to be with a boy to do that.

I carried a strong sense that I was different throughout adolescence. I knew I could be happy just being with my girlfriends, and boys seemed unnecessary, even bothersome. I had a boyfriend in sixth grade, until I broke up with him when I found out that he had a lot of set ideas on what I was supposed to do just because I was his girlfriend, like going to football games and giving him Donovan records. I didn't like that, and after I broke up with him, I was done with being involved with boys for a long time. I had a few crushes on boys, but generally they all bored me, and I preferred writing intense notes back and forth with my girlfriends and talking for hours on the phone after school to being part of the boy-girl chase.

When I was fourteen, I fell in love with my best friend and 1 began to wonder if I was a lesbian. I had read about lesbians in Mary McCarthy's *The Group*. I wanted to spend all of my time with her, and I dropped several friends because they paled beside the excitement that I felt when I was with her. When we walked down State Street after school browsing in bookstores, spent hours listening to Joan Baez or Arlo Guthrie records, danced to Beatles records, planned our lives, and shared everything we knew, I felt more in tune with her than I had ever felt with anybody. When we walked together through the halls of school or on the way home, sharing secrets, I felt like our bodies were in complete synchronization.

She was my best friend even after I moved away to Albany, New York, and I spent much of high school writing her letters, single-spaced typewritten letters seventeen pages long. I lived with a passion for her return letters. When I would come home from school and find one of her thick letters in a long envelope with her artistic handwriting on it, I would run upstairs until dinner, not wanting to be with anybody but her. I yearned for those vacations when I was able to go back to Madison to see her or she would come east and we could spend time in person. I didn't date, but spent a lot of time with a church youth group and worked on progressive political campaigns, and my emotional life centered on her and other women friends.

When I went to college in Massachusetts in 1973, I began to take women's studies courses. A friend commented that the only thing I seemed truly excited about studying was women. I went to spend that summer in Albany and took an intensive women's studies course that met every morning. Every afternoon I wrote pages in my journal and read all the books and articles on the "more than required reading" list. I encountered many out lesbians from Albany in that class, older women in their late twenties and thirties, many taking this course when the lesbian community was just beginning to surface in Albany. We talked openly about sexuality, homophobia, and conflicts between lesbians and straight women. The professor was a lesbian who was very outspoken about the pain of having been closeted.

I became very caught up in the class and got a crush on one of the other women. When I returned to college that fall, I announced to my friends that I had a crush on a lesbian and was bisexual.

When I was twenty-one, I took a year off from college and moved to Boston, where I became involved with my first male lover. One of the major reasons I was drawn to him was that he knew about and supported my bisexuality, which strengthened our bond. I knew I was going to have women lovers at some time in my life. I thought a lot then about ways of being involved with both women and men, emotionally and sexually, and differences in relationships with people of different genders.

In Boston, the lesbian and feminist community was thriving and reading, thinking, and talking a lot about feminism and sex roles. In 1978, I went to my first gay pride march, because I was interested to see what it was like, and I felt proud and excited to be there. I wondered if people thought I was a lesbian, even though I was there with a man, and felt pleased by that prospect.

Being bisexual, with women as close friends but still sleeping with men, changed after I broke up with my last male lover in 1979. I was still bisexual for a couple of years, but any desire to be involved with men soon abated. I had an affair with a good friend from the Women's Center and fell in love with her, although she moved away from Boston. We spent hours staring at each other in meetings, hours leafleting dark streets for the feminist campaign we worked on, and hours in bed and on my living room sofa, drinking white wine and arguing about separatism and how you could exist in this world without men. Those discussions were an integral part of my coming out as a lesbian. Having sex with her was very easy and natural. I felt *loving* toward her in a way I had not with men.

I still considered myself bisexual, until one Saturday afternoon in 1981 at a feminist forum at a university in Boston. Everything that had been building within for years, growing toward coming out, rushed to a head that day. I looked deeply into the eyes of a woman I had long admired, a lesbian activist in her midthirties whom I knew through my political work. I knew for sure that I was a lesbian and that she knew too. I looked closely at her a second time, feeling another wave of recognition and mutual interest, and again a third time for a long, slow stare full of energy and desire. Then, I looked shyly away, until finally I looked a fourth time with a sense of firm connection, knowing, *Yes, we are in this life together.* She never became my lover, and in fact, what I had felt standing before her was so intense, I felt awkward around her for a long time after that. The years of questioning and the simmering consciousness that I was a lesbian erupted in me in that moment when I knew there was no going back. She became a role model for me. I was fascinated by the sight of her and by being in the same room with her, every detail about her was etched with a significance I had not felt before. I felt more excitement and energy for life than I had felt before coming out. I would think about her all the time, in meetings, at work, in conjunction with books I was reading. I would think of her whenever I had an interesting perception or observation. She was not the only woman on my mind those days, but she was the beacon and in my head and heart the most.

After I came out, I became much more aware of homophobia. I had always sensed it in others, and in myself, although I didn't always have the words to describe it. My images of lesbians during high school and college were positive – compelling, appealing, and romantic – but I felt scared to go toward other lesbians. I sensed that lesbian relationships weren't approved of, and my images of lesbians contrasted with the admonitions I received from my parents when I didn't act "feminine" enough, which was often. I was never the lady I was raised to be. When I grew older and read feminist literature and *Gay Community News,* I began to know well the slights, oppression, and discrimination that lesbians experience. This knowledge didn't make it easier to come out, although those same books and newspapers offered me an essential connection to the community. For a while, being bisexual and holding out the possibility of getting involved with a man gave me a cushion of heterosexual privilege which I wasn't ready to give up. I didn't know how my parents or old friends would take the news that I was a lesbian, or the possible discriminations I would face. But as time went on, describing myself as bisexual felt more and more unauthentic, and it became clear to me that I was more strongly committed and connected to women.

Coming out also brought me closer to a feeling of community than I had ever felt before, yet at the same time I was aware of my difference from heterosexist culture. I felt that what I was experiencing was so intensely personal (although I was fully aware of the political aspects of being a lesbian) that I wanted time within myself and with close friends and lovers to explore my passions for women. Every day during my lunch hour and over weekends, I hungrily read lesbian/feminist and gay literature, Adrienne Rich, Marilyn Frye, and every book that Persephone Press ever published. Those years were socially very separatist for me. My social and political life revolved around women, lesbians, but I also kept up a number of important friendships with straight and bisexual women, and a couple of male friends from college. I felt a great deal of sureness and relief in coming out, and felt like I could do almost anything. Being closeted to my parents and at work was hard, and I felt the contradictions between straight people's assumptions of who I was and my own knowledge and sense of myself; but the joy, power, and rightness I felt in coming out has made it worth the long process.

Marcie Just

Sharpshooter

Another school year was beginning and with it the transfer to senior high. It was 1965 in East St. Louis and my primary concerns were thoughts of teachers, classmates, and new friends. I was making my first attempt at learning a foreign language, and had chosen Spanish.

Spanish class was only a short stroll down the hall from my homeroom, so I was one of the first to arrive. I took a seat at the back of the classroom so I could check out the others as they arrived. All the faces were new, but one in particular caught my eye. There was something about her. I noted how well her dark blue sweater contrasted with her brown hair. My eyes followed her as she took a seat close to mine.

Soon the teacher arrived and called the class to order. "I am Miss Santos," she informed us. She took the seat behind her desk. "As I call each of your names, please tell something about yourself." She glanced at the list of students. "Barbara Andrews," she called, and looked out at the class. The girl who had caught my eye raised her hand.

"I'm a junior and assistant captain of the cheerleading squad," she said proudly in a musical voice.

I found it hard to concentrate on the others and kept glancing at Barbara and wondering what she was like. When my name was called, I raised my hand. Barbara looked around, and our eyes met. All thoughts were driven from my mind. After what seemed like a long time, I managed to bring my thoughts under control. "I'm a sophomore," I stammered.

Miss Santos smiled. "I don't often have sophomores in my classes," she said. "Why did you decide to take it this year?"

"I've wanted to study Spanish since I was in sixth grade, so I decided to take it as soon as I could," I answered. Miss Santos smiled again, then glanced down at her list.

I looked again at Barbara and found her smiling at me. I smiled back, then looked away before anyone else could notice. My heart was beating faster. I wanted to sing! But I also felt confused. I had been told that feelings like these were what I would feel for a man. I quickly decided I should put Barbara out of my mind and not give her another thought.

Gym was my last class of the day and I welcomed the break from academia. I was sitting on the last step of the bleachers watching the class assemble, when Barbara walked in carrying her orange-and-blue pom-poms. She glanced about and saw me sitting there. She waved at me, smiled, and then made her way to the locker room.

A woman sitting next to me asked, "Do you know her?"

"She's in my Spanish class," I said, trying to sound casual.

"The cheerleaders practice during the last hour," she said, answering my unspoken question.

Barbara would be in the locker room at the same time as I was. That thought made the strange feelings return. I tried to shove thoughts of her aside, but I kept seeing her face in my mind.

As the term progressed, I found myself waiting impatiently for Spanish class, so I could hear her voice as she recited. Then I couldn't wait for gym class. Occasionally, while dressing for gym, I would catch a glimpse of her bare shoulder just before she slipped into her cheerleader sweater, or see her dressed only in bra and panties as she changed back to her street clothes. As I finished dressing, I would imagine caressing her and feeling her softness and warmth. I wanted to run my hands through her short, brown hair and hear her speak my name. During this very turbulent and emotional time, I learned a name for what I was.

◆

A new neighbor had moved in across the street. She wasn't like most of the women in the neighborhood. I watched her for a while, trying to figure her out. The neighborhood women wore dresses and were usually shepherding children. She always wore slacks, men's shirts, and work boots. She was often alone, and seemed to keep to herself. I imagined she must be lonely.

One day I decided to go over and introduce myself. I felt a bit timid as I knocked on her door, not knowing how she would react to my being there. As I waited for her to answer, it occurred to me that maybe she liked being alone. As I thought of going back home, she came to the door. She opened it wide and stepped out onto the porch. I had to look up to meet her eyes, and felt relief that they held welcome.

"I'm a neighbor," I said. "I live in the white house across the street."

She looked across the street and nodded. Her gaze turned back to me.

"I'm Nora," she said, extending her hand.

"Marcie," I said as I shook it.

"Would you like to come in?" she asked.

I nodded.

She closed the door behind us. "Have a seat," she said, motioning toward the flowered couch. "Can I get you a soda?"

"Yes, ma'am. I'd like that," I answered.

As she walked toward her kitchen, I realized how ridiculous her large body would look in the kind of dresses the women in the neighborhood wore. Besides, she seemed comfortable dressing the way she did.

She returned with the soda, handed it to me, then seated herself in one of the chairs.

"Are you in high school? You look about that age," she said.

"I'm a sophomore," I replied, and took a drink of the soda.

She nodded. "I guess you'd like to know something about me," she said, half-amused.

"I admit I'm curious," I answered.

"I was a nurse during the Korean War, and then chose to pursue a career in the army," she explained. "I retired recently and decided to come back home."

Momentarily there was a look in her eyes that I couldn't understand, but she continued her story before I could think about it.

"When I went to East Saint Louis Senior High, it was a small building downtown. Nothing like the nice school you go to."

We were quiet for a moment, then she said, "I'd like to show you something. I'll be right back."

She returned with what appeared to be a picture frame. She sat next to me on the couch.

"These are my sharpshooter medals," she said proudly. "That one," she said, pointing to a miniature rifle, "I won when I outshot every man on the field."

"Wow, are you still that good?" I asked.

"I got a five-point buck last winter," she boasted.

I didn't know what a five-point buck was, but she was proud of it. I smiled broadly.

"The other medals aren't very impressive," she said. She set them aside. "Now tell me about you." Her brown eyes showed genuine interest.

"I'm the fifth oldest of ten children, and the oldest one at home now. My interests range from reading and playing guitar to coaching a softball team. I like to play volleyball, too."

Then she asked the question I dreaded most. "Do you have a boyfriend?"

"No," I answered honestly. "Most of the guys want to talk about cars, and frankly, I'm not interested."

To my surprise, she smiled, and nodded as if she had already figured I didn't.

Thoughts of Barbara came to mind, and I suddenly wanted to run, before she could know what I was thinking. I stood and said, "Nora, I have to go now and help Mom with dinner, but I'll be back."

Her eyes held mine with a measuring stare, but she didn't try to stop me.

"Come anytime. I've enjoyed our talk."

"Thanks for the soda," I said as she saw me to the door. I almost ran home. Somehow Nora seemed to know something about me, and I wasn't entirely comfortable with that thought.

I rushed into the house and found my mother in the kitchen. Standing in the doorway, I told her about Nora.

"Mom, I met our new neighbor. Her name is Nora. She is a retired army nurse, and has sharpshooter medals too. Nora got a five-point buck last winter," I said all in one breath.

Mother gave a look of warning, and glanced in the direction of the living room.

In my enthusiasm to share my information about Nora, I had rushed by without seeing my father.

He made a disapproving sound, and rustled the newspaper. "Hunting is not for women," he said gruffly. "The mannish bitch ought to get herself a husband." The newspaper rustled again.

I turned to make a comment, and felt my mother's restraining grip on my arm. "Will you peel the potatoes?" she asked gently.

Before I had the chance to talk with Nora again, I discovered something about her. Nora had a lady friend. At least once a week, her bright green Chevrolet was parked in front of Nora's house. My first impression of her was that she must be a professional of some sort, as she usually wore skirts and matching jackets.

I looked forward to seeing Nora after her friend had visited. She always seemed so happy then. The sadness in her eyes, that I believed must have come from being a nurse during the Korean War, would be replaced with joy. We never spoke of the other woman, so I never learned her name or anything about her.

One evening when my father came home from work, I could tell by the noise he was making that he was in a bad mood. I wished in vain that I was upstairs safely in my bedroom, but unfortunately I was in the kitchen. I braced myself as he stormed into the room. He headed for the refrigerator and got a beer. He took a long swallow, then sighed. By the way he stood I knew he was mad about something. I glanced over at my mother. She was drying her hands on a towel. "Supper will be ready soon, dear. Why don't you read the paper while you wait," she said soothingly.

He took another drink, then crushed the can.

"You never see her with a man," he said. "And she's always dressed like one." His contempt was plain in the tone of his voice. "Mannish bitch."

I didn't have to ask who he meant, and Mother's silence seemed to indicate she knew as well.

"Every time you turn around that blonde bitch is over there. I wonder what those queers do in bed," he said contemptuously as he turned and left the kitchen.

"I'll be right back," I told my mother, and went upstairs to my room. My thoughts raced as I sat there hearing his words repeat in my mind. I wanted to talk to Nora. I wanted to know if she felt for the blonde lady what I felt for Barbara.

At dinner my father was still in a sullen mood. I kept my eyes on my plate and desperately tried to avoid calling his attention to me. Just when I thought we'd get through dinner without a tirade, he dropped the bombshell. "Marcie, I don't want you to go over there," he said in a tone that indicated no argument was possible. "I don't want you near that queer, again. Is that understood?"

I lifted my eyes to look at him as I answered, "Yes, sir." A look of hatred was in his eyes. I never visited Nora again, nor did I find anyone during high school to share my feelings with.

◆

In college the game seemed to accept more diversity in its players, and amidst this freedom I found courage.

I met her in the fall of 1970, during my junior year at Southern Illinois University. I was in the cafeteria of the student union, struggling over the material for a quiz in geography.

Mary Lou flipped into the chair across from me. "Another map quiz?" she asked solicitously.

"Yeah," I said and looked up. Next to Mary Lou sat a woman wrapped in a green cape. Her long, blonde hair cascaded over it. She leaned over the table and looked curiously at the map for a moment.

Mary Lou chose that moment to introduce us. "Louise, this is Marcie," she said, and we all turned quickly back to the map.

Louise was a whiz. She made sense out of squiggles that were rivers. Lakes, forests, and mountains were clearly visible to her eyes. I was impressed.

She was not what others would call beautiful. She was short and round, and had a square, heavy-featured face. But I saw a beauty and power in her that strongly attracted me.

We talked often after that and discovered our mutual love of music and sports. Her blue eyes would sparkle as we discussed the exploits of our favorite hockey player. That winter her parents took a ski vacation, and she invited me to stay with her while they were gone. The house sat apart from the others on the lane, at the edge of a forest. The tranquil setting soon worked its magic, and we began to relax.

Late one afternoon, after our classes, we came to the house. I put an album on the turntable as she prepared dinner. I built a fire, and sat down in front of it. Shortly, she joined me. "Dinner won't need my attention for a while," she said, making herself comfortable next to me.

I turned and our eyes met. At that moment I wanted to kiss her, but was too shy to make a move. She sensed my desire and moved closer. Our lips met, our hands explored, and we made love. For both of us it was the first time with a woman. Our joy was so welcome, yet so strange. It wasn't so much a conscious choice as it was a realization. It felt so right to love a woman, yet we felt guilt and shame for having tasted the forbidden fruit.

Even though we decided not to tell anyone, our actions spoke clearly. We spent every free moment together. Our happiness spilled out without conscious knowledge. Even though friends started acting strangely and conversation would cease when we entered a room, I knew I could not stop caring for her. I had taken the step and would never go back.

Pam McArthur

Spring, Finally

Spring has come to us finally and I cannot write. The garden has its needs; the fields and woods, their pleasures. Brisk, dewy mornings find me on my knees, digging and planting. Clear afternoons call me into the woods, where the buds are bursting on the trees and the air is thick with long-awaited birds. Following a bright flash of orange, I find an oriole building his pouchy nest high in the branches of an oak; pheasants squawk in the undergrowth. Come evening — my usual time for writing — I am bone-weary and too content to wrestle with language, to try to put words to the feelings flowing at the edge of my consciousness. Yet I will try, for spring is the perfect backdrop for this story, with its exuberance of lilac and forsythia, the hidden beauty of pink-edged lady's slipper; this immersion in the world of the senses.

Sweet. This is the first and best word that comes to me when I think of first falling in love, some twenty years ago. Sweet, those months of growing closer, till I breathed in the warm scent of her skin with every breath I took. Sweet, the naïve uncertainty that kept me trembling, not knowing what I wanted, not knowing if she would want it, too. And sweet, the touch of feather-shy fingers gradually growing bolder in their wanting.

I want to be clear that the beginning felt like pure love. I want to be clear, because that love was assailed from the very start by the pain of secrecy, then by my parents' unrelenting disapproval, and, finally, by my own insecurity and homophobia. It is a miracle to me that the sweetness we knew survived for as long as it did.

We were sixteen, seventeen, when it all started. Her name was Peg, and she lived next door. Already we were different from most of the other girls. We spent our time reading horse books and galloping through the woods behind our houses, neighing and kicking up our heels. Weekend nights we spent together, laying down a nest of blankets and sleeping bags on the floor so we could read and talk late into the night. One night she held my hand. It took me hours to fall asleep, and when I woke, her hand was still in mine.

I was very shy about this touching. We never talked about it, and I never knew if it meant as much to her as it did to me. I couldn't bring myself to take the next step – I didn't know what the next step was! For months I bumped into her "accidentally," hoping she didn't mind, thrilled at even this slight touch. Finally, we began to turn toward each other, slowly discovering the delights and passions of our bodies, taking all the time we needed, and making everything up as we went along. I was enthralled; I was ecstatic. I was not good at hiding my desires. Before long, my parents figured out what was happening.

My mother came to my room one night. Without preamble she said, "You must stop being so ... intimate ... with Peg." My world collapsed under her disapproval. Each day of the next year was filled with tension created by the fear and guilt of knowing my parents hated what I was doing, even while being with Peg felt absolutely right to me. The thrill of sexuality long held back and the desperate defiance I used as a shield added to the pressure.

In the beginning of my senior year in high school, my parents sent me to a psychiatrist. The message was clear: they wanted me fixed. The psychiatrist was noncommittal about my homosexuality – neither passing judgment nor giving support. He did, however, recommend that my parents give me a bit more breathing space. This was a relief, although tensions still ran high in the house.

I remember vividly the long minutes I spent almost every day on the landing of our staircase – halfway between the safety of my bedroom and the judgment of my parents in the living room. Caught between desire and fear, angry at both Peg and my parents for putting me in this position, I would gather up my courage, take the final steps, and say, "I'm going over to Peg's house." I would be met with stony silence and my mother's pleading eyes. I never knew on which days, pushed beyond her limits, she would say something. Things like:

Where did I go wrong?
We shouldn't have sent you to that all-girls school.
I'll believe it if you're still like this when you turn thirty.
I'll give you a dollar for every day you don't see Peg.
Where did I go wrong?

And my father – where was he while this was going on? As I remember it, he left most of the child-rearing to my mother, which was a shame. We could have used more of his quiet philosophy and humor to ease the tension between mother and daughter – twin souls of stubborn self-righteousness. But he is a background figure in my memory of this time, and while he struggled to understand me, my father seemed to side with my mother in thinking that homosexuality was wrong and hoping that I would outgrow this "phase."

My heart was wrenched between my long-standing loyalty to my parents and this newfound love for and loyalty to Peg. I didn't know how to answer my mother's arguments. I had never heard anything to support my belief that my love was both acceptable and beautiful; defending myself was like trying to walk the air between a canyon's walls. I had to build a tightrope of anger and defiance just to survive.

My parents' constant disapproval began to wear me down. I began to doubt I was truly in love. I lay in bed at night, whispering into the darkness: *I love her — I don't love her*. I could not tell which was true. Finally, I decided that I loved Peg for her essence, her spirit — I would've loved her even if she had been a man. I could not reconcile the wonder of loving Peg with the isolation and shame I associated with being gay, so I had to convince myself we were special, not really gay, but living some sort of transcendent love.

Even more disturbing was that, having repeatedly been told that what I deeply believed in was wrong, I began to feel dirty. I took that feeling in under my skin. I had a physical sensation of dirt on my hands, and believed that I would soil anything I touched. Any friendship, any undertaking, would be ruined if I were a part of it. I still feel the anguish of that time, even now, twenty years later. I still fear rejection every time I come out to someone; I still assume that that person will not accept, will not be comfortable with, who I am. The young woman who battled with confusion and self-hatred is still a part of me, despite all the changes over these twenty years.

And there have been many changes. I went away to college and encountered feminism and gay liberation. For the first time I met people who gave me support, people who encouraged me to be open and proud of being a lesbian. I also became a writer and began writing the stories and poems of my own life, acknowledging and celebrating the world I know. My long relationship with Peg, which sustained me through much of this, finally ended, but I learned that life sometimes gives you a second chance at love. I am now happily entering middle age. I live with my lover, Beth — eight years, this winter! — and our son, Aaron, who has changed our lives in ways I can't even begin to describe.

Through all the changes, the process of coming out has skipped and jumped like the thread of a poorly woven fabric. It is a process that will be with me till the day I die. It is not something I am always comfortable doing, but it is the only option my pride allows me. And I find myself thinking about this more and more since I've become a mother. It is imperative to me that Aaron never be ashamed of his family — his wonderful two-mom family — and I can make that possible for him only by example. As we meet the world — other parents at the playground, strangers in the grocery store — I explain our family, and in doing so I feel I am making it easier for us. I am saying that I am proud of our lives. My life.

Rising early this morning, Aaron and I go into the yard as usual. The sun is hot already — spring leaping into summer. We fill the birdfeeder with plump seeds to beckon the cardinals and chickadees, the grosbeak with his sunburst splash of red at the throat. Aaron, not yet two years old, delights in calling, "Come and get it, birds!" Then he takes my hand and leads me to the flower bed. Exuberantly, he yells, "The poppies are beautiful! The peonies are great!" as he gently reaches one fingertip out to touch a bursting ball of flower. I am thrilled to see this in him, to see how natural it is for this child to love the earth and all things he meets on it. I vow to encourage him always to respect and love the earth; and most importantly, I promise to teach him about difference. I hope that, knowing that his family is different, yet wonderful, knowing that his moms are different, yet proud of our lives, he will never be afraid of difference in himself or others; never hide his own unique light, never reject it in others. This is my gift to my son. It is part of my healing of the hurt young woman still inside me. And it is the hope I offer to the future.

Karen Barber

Pat Robertson Had a Point*

"**K**aren has a da-ate, Karen has a da-ate," one of my roommates sang as she danced around our apartment.

It was a cold Friday the thirteenth in March 1987, my senior year at Boston College; the moon was full. There were six of us living in our three-bedroom campus apartment, and we were all preparing to go out for the night. Although I often accompanied my friends to off-campus parties on the weekends, this night was different: tonight, I was catching dinner and a movie with Susan-the-lesbian.

Dressed in black from head to toe, I continued to apply eyeliner as Joann bopped around the apartment, tormenting me. There was nothing hostile in her words; it was good-natured ribbing, and I snickered at her comments along with my roommates. Susan and I were friends spending the evening together; I had nothing to hide.

---

* when, in 1992, he described feminism as "a Socialist, anti-family political movement that encourages women to leave their husbands, kill their children, practice witchcraft, destroy capitalism, and become lesbians."

Finally, I was ready to go. On my way out, I innocently asked Joann if she had some gum. "Why, are you going to kiss her?" was her reply. I smirked and went on my way.

◆

Susan and I met in Introduction to Feminism during the first semester of our junior year. It was a student-taught course, and I was taking it with three friends. I had never seen Susan before, but it took only that first class to know that we'd end up — at the very least — in bed together. In a sea of pearls, blonde bobs, and cardigans, Susan, with her nose-ring and unshaven legs, was a radical. A radical lesbian-feminist. And I wanted to know her.

I always tell people I was born a feminist. A tomboy growing up, I was the first girl in my hometown in New Jersey to try out for Little League. My next-door neighbor was a coach, and after the tryouts, he told my father that I was certainly good enough for the league. When I didn't make it, I knew that I wouldn't be playing that summer only because I was a girl. I knew then that life wasn't fair, and that life as a feminist was going to be a challenge.

As a kid, my actions constituted my feminism. During high school and college, my feminism became more cerebral. I read newspapers; I read feminist theory. And I talked about women and injustice whenever I had the chance. In high school, few cared; in college, my audience of friends and classmates was more sympathetic, although one roommate's boyfriend was scared to be around when I was reading anything by Mary Daly.

I can't explain how I knew so quickly and so surely that Susan and I would end up together. Susan was easily the most knowledgeable student in the class, and I was drawn to her intellect. I found her discussions stimulating and, among women who were decidedly not feminists, refreshing. And when I took my attraction to Susan's mind a step further, when I realized that I might be sexual with Susan, I wasn't filled with anxiety, pain, or guilt. I wasn't horrified; I wasn't disgusted; I was looking forward to it. Without feminism, I don't think I would have been so comfortable with the idea.

There was Kevin to think about, though. Kevin and I had been going together since sophomore year. He was a sweet guy, and I loved him. I liked his friends, he liked mine, and the two groups soon merged into one. Deep down, though, I knew I wasn't going to spend the rest of my life with Kevin. Something I couldn't quite put my finger on was missing from our relationship. I was attracted to Kevin, but there wasn't any spark, any fire. Our lovemaking lacked passion. On the other hand, I was excited by the idea of being with Susan. I began to worry that I was being unfair to Kevin, that I was using him to be "normal." I started to wonder if I had been gay all along. Was I hiding behind him, as well as behind previous boy-friends, suppressing my lesbian desires to fit in? It was a hard question to answer. Growing up, I was never tortured by unrequited love for my girlfriends. When I was little, I played mostly with the neighborhood boys; girls, with their giggling and frilly dresses, didn't interest me. I do remember playing "motorcycles" on our bikes with one girl who lived a few houses down. Since girls didn't ride motorcycles, we pretended to be boys, and even drew "girlie" calendars to hang in the garage for the appropriate atmosphere. She's a dyke now, too. When I think back, the women who in retrospect were obviously lesbian – a gym teacher here, a softball umpire there – intrigued me. I admired their independence, their toughness, their butchness. I thought they were cool, and I thought I was like them. But as I reached puberty, I chose to kiss boys. I liked it, but making out with boys didn't thrill me. And because, for the most part, there were no fireworks, I decided then that sex was overrated, and I — being less concerned with carnal pleasures — was simply more evolved than the average teen.

◆

Introduction to Feminism was one of many classes Susan and I took together. We were both working toward a minor in women's studies and there were few courses offered. At times, four of my five classes were women's studies courses — most with Susan. In addition, Susan and a few others on campus were forming a feminist group, Womynfire. I like to think I helped with that, although I really just showed up for meetings with a few of my roommates. So, besides seeing Susan almost every day, I was now seeing her many nights, as well. I was doubting my sexuality and spending a lot of time with one of the first out lesbians I knew, who was cute, smart, and single. How could we not end up together? But, for now, I was still straight; I had Kevin.

Senior year, while I lived on campus, Susan lived off campus, sharing a house with at least two gay men and, at any given time, one other lesbian. One of her roommates was big-fag-on-campus; one of her best friends was big-dyke-on-campus. Between her friends and the women I met in my classes, I soon realized that, Catholic or not, Boston College had a substantial gay community.

Second semester, senior year, something had to give. I was growing more and more attracted to Susan, and the sense of outrage I was feeling toward men was taking a toll on my relationship with Kevin. I broke up with him on Valentine's Day. I can't remember what I told him, probably something

---

103

vague about not being able to reconcile my politics and my feelings. He was hurt, and I remember him asking if that meant I was going to spend my life alone. I didn't answer him. (And while I was breaking up with Kevin, Susan was seeing Holly Near in concert with a straight girlfriend. When Susan admitted that she had a crush on me, her friend said, "Karen? She's straight!!" Susan told her not to be so sure.)

Kevin and I remained friends, while Susan and I began spending more time together. We took trips to Cambridge to shop at New Words, the feminist bookstore. She even took me to Somewhere Else, then Boston's only lesbian bar.

◆

One Friday afternoon, not long after our "date," Susan invited me over for tea. I couldn't stay long, I told her, a friend from high school was coming into town, and my roommates and I were throwing a party that night. She greeted me at the door. I think she was shaking. After what seemed a lifetime of small talk, she finally announced that she had a crush on me and thought I should know. I panicked. I babbled something about just breaking up with Kevin and not wanting to be in a relationship, and so on and so on. "Calm down," she said, "I *like* you, I don't want to *marry* you." I left, thrilled but scared, went home, and proceeded to get very, very drunk, making a fool of myself at the party. While drunk, I even called Susan and invited her to the party. Put off by my drunkenness, she declined. I was sick for days. When I showed up late for our Monday Women and Philosophy class, looking sick and haggard, she thought she had destroyed me with her revelation.

We first kissed on April Fool's Day. For days after that, Susan was convinced that I was going to call her up and say, "April Fool's!" But it was no joke; my life had changed. I didn't tell any of my roommates about my relationship with Susan. I don't think they would have rejected me, but I decided that since we were graduating in less than two months, why rock the boat? Susan always said I picked her when I did because it was easy: I could have the experience of sleeping with a woman, graduate, leave the state, and never have to deal with it again. That's true, I guess, but I didn't factor in our falling in love.

Our time together, before the school year ended, was short. We made love at her house, but I would never stay the night. I might leave at three in the morning, but by God, I wasn't going to raise suspicion by not coming home at all. I learned later that my roommates routinely debated my behavior; they weren't stupid, but while most suspected what was going on, they never let on.

Senior Week, just before graduation, was tense. I had to balance my time between my roommates, my friends, and Susan. I went to Gatsby Night with my friends, then spent two blissful days in Provincetown with Susan. I went to the clambake with my roommates, hiding when I ran into some new lesbian friends. One night I did both: I spent the early part of an evening in bed with Susan, then got up, got dressed, and went to Beers 'n' Tears with guess who? Hanging out with Kevin et al., smelling like Susan, wasn't easy. Susan actually came to this one event; seeing her in this context — blurring the line between my two lives — made me dizzy.

We graduated in mid-May. Susan stayed in Boston, and I returned to New Jersey with my family. What followed was one of the most difficult summers of my life. We were tortured lovers, ripped apart just as we were beginning to fall in love. Never having written a love note before, we wrote every day: long letters or silly notes. I sent cassette tapes to Susan, filled with songs that reminded me of her. She'd send beautiful, hand-painted cards. More practically, she sent me *Sojourner* and the Help Wanted section of the *Boston Globe* so that I could find a job and move back up there. We cried. We spoke on the phone when we could. And these new feelings scared me almost as much as they excited me. I had never felt this way about a boy.

I visited her once that summer — the weekend of gay pride, a disastrous encounter fueled by alcohol and the pressure of jamming everything we wanted to do and say into two days. I arrived one afternoon unannounced; I phoned her house from around the corner to make sure she was home, talked to her briefly, then told her I had to run. I was on her doorstep, ringing her bell, in less than a minute. We immediately fell into bed, without taking the time to collect ourselves and reconnect. We were shocked and confused to find our lovemaking awkward and forced. It set the tone for the weekend. The next day was the pride parade. Convinced that I would appear on the front page of the *Boston Globe,* or worse yet, on the cover of a national news magazine, I refused to go. Susan, of course, was hurt. A week's worth of gut-wrenching letters set things straight.

In September, I secured a six-week, unpaid internship with a Boston publishing company. I arranged to stay with two straight friends from BC who had a small two-bedroom apartment outside the city. I shared a double bed with Kathy — who claims now to have pegged me on my first night at Boston College. She and Stephanie shared a room even then, and that first night, I kept them up talking into the night. When I left, Kathy turned to Stephanie and said, "She's a lesbian, although she may not know it yet."

Since Susan and I were living on opposite sides of Boston, without a car, we worked out a schedule of meeting after work for a drink at Somewhere Else. Every so often, I'd pack an overnight bag and stay with her. One night in October, Adrienne Rich was scheduled to read her poetry in Cambridge. Susan wanted to go, as did Stephanie. Technically, I wasn't out to Steph and Kathy, and Susan made it clear that she was not going to pretend that we were "just friends," especially among all the lesbians who would be at the reading. I agreed that there was no reason to hide, and decided that I would talk to Steph at dinner before the reading. So, at Pizzeria Uno in Harvard Square, I first told someone that I was a lesbian. I picked the right person to come out to; Steph, of course, already knew.

◆

After convincing myself that this wasn't a phase, I came out to my parents, by letter, some year and a half after Susan and I first kissed. Prior to that, I had been driving one of my housemates crazy with coming-out-to-my-parents worst-case scenarios. My brother had just announced that he was getting married, and I ranted and raved that my lover would never be welcomed into our family with the same enthusiasm that my future sister-in-law was. "The injustice!" I screamed; "The bigotry!" I cried. "Shut up!" said my housemate. "You don't know how they are going to react; don't they deserve a chance to prove you wrong?" Reluctantly, I agreed. I wrote a long letter, explaining my relationship with Susan, the choices I had made. Over and over again, I stressed how happy I was and that they had nothing to worry about. They had raised me right and given me the strength to be who I am; if anything they should be proud.

A few days after receiving the letter, my father called. I was shocked at his reaction. He talked about, among other things, religion (I never knew just how Catholic he was!), homosexuals' being unfit to teach children, and the dangers of being gay in today's world — look at what happened to Harvey Milk, he said! Although impressed that he knew who Harvey Milk was, I was appalled at his conservatism, his disapproval. To this day, my mother and I have never talked about my being a lesbian.

Now, I'm out to all of my friends from college, and all of my high school friends with whom I am still in contact. Since college graduation, I've worked only in jobs where queers were in the majority. A stint at a video store taught me that my attraction was to women, not just to Susan. One of the two dyke managers introduced me to the fine art of lesbian cruising; watching her, I learned how to appreciate, and flirt with, cute girls.

I like being a lesbian. And I like lesbians. My heart and my politics belong to women; I would have it no other way.

Judith McDaniel

Ten Years of Change

Fragments: At the Beginning

(1965, Exeter University, England, journal notes)

3 May: Carolyn and I were discussing my novel — she really takes it quite to heart — I suggested at one point that the "slow, steady woman" should in reality be a lesbian, and I thought she was going to call out her lawyers. It helps me, though, to take my writing seriously, because she does ... Tonight I remembered a moment from last fall at Stratford: two Japanese girls — quite sophisticated-looking, but young — holding tightly to each other's hand, one leading, one following — as they worked their way up the theater steps. A longing pang — not allowed in Western culture.

5 May: I want her respect — hers and others'— which is the only reason I'm trying to organize my life. It's not easy, but it's worth it. I don't love many people.

12 May: We were talking about letters this afternoon and how to sign them, etc. Anyway, she said there were only three possible ways to close ... "Yours faithfully," "Yours sincerely," and "Love from." I asked which category I was in, and she said, "Oh, you're different." Don't know what that meant, but she said in the future I'll get a "Love from."

17 May: I had some funny ups and downs today. I guess it was from sitting at my desk and working ... then Carolyn was going out and I wasn't, which still galls occasionally. I went in to see Carolyn for a few minutes this afternoon. She had three exams this week, and I knew she'd be busy, but she said so, too – something to the effect of "Well, you'll be on your own for the next three days, you know." Well, I did, but don't like to be reminded of it – nor of the fact that in four more weeks I'll be on my own for good. So I indulged in being depressed and went and had my bath and came back when who should come rapping on the door. I hadn't gone in to say good night to her, because the light was off, so I knew she must have gotten out of bed to say good night ... and that made all the difference. I could have sung.

22 May: Carolyn and I sat and talked all afternoon. She started out calling me names. I didn't really mind, because it's gotten to the point now that for my own preservation I can't afford to believe she's serious. Anyway, at some point I told her how hard it had been for me to watch her and Geoff together – which brought her up short. It's funny knowing someone so well you can say that and know the precise effect it will have. Then we talked about us and how chancy any sort of attempt to establish communication was ... but we seemed to have been successful and, god, it's going to be hard to leave.

23 May: We talked all day again today. I've never felt so close to anyone. At times I think – panic – exams – and then I think, But does it really matter? Obviously, not that much ... We went flower picking tonight under the cover of darkness — one of the lesser social sins — it was cold and raining. Brought back lily of the valley, lilac, straw flowers, and some other sprays ... there seemed to be a marked predominance of white ... except for the first rose of summer Carolyn found on a vine and put in the small vase for me — it's pink.

Fragments: Denial

1971, on waking in Jon's bed, a dream: In a kind of a girl's dorm. I am standing with my friend in our room. Across the hall from my room is a bathroom with several stalls. For a while I am inside one of them or else I know what is inside one of them, as I am still across the hall in my room. I keep urging my friend to hurry. Just then someone discovers the girl's body — she is dead. They say she was murdered, but it's my dream and I know it was suicide. I won't go look at her, but I know what she looks like. Now I tell my friend I want to leave quick before the police come or we'll have to wait longer. But she says no, it wouldn't be right. So they come with a stretcher to get the body, but there's not much left. She killed herself by chopping off pieces — a bit at a time — and putting them in the toilet.

1972, July, a self-conscious fantasy: Sometimes I think I would like to have an affair with a woman. I don't know why — it's not curiosity — but I think that something is lacking emotionally in all of my relationships.

1972, October, journal notes: Driving home alone from hearing Adrienne Rich read her poems. She is a force, an intensity, and affects me profoundly. There are many dimensions to her poems. I want to read them over and over. "Can you dig it, baby" on the radio. I feel a sense of loss when I hear poetry like that. Because she is writing for me and I understand her in a way I have never understood the "great" poets — Yeats, Eliot, etc. Why loss? There must be men who read Yeats and to whom he means as much, perhaps more, than this night meant to me. And I'd never really thought about it, but — she exposes herself in her work and I feel I know her well, like I should be driving home with her. But no man in that audience should feel *just* the way I do — something, perhaps, because her clarity is good — but not exactly as I felt. She is totally honest, but you have to have been there to know the truth.

1973, August, journal notes: I told Phyllis how I felt about Sue, making it sound as though I was horrified and terrified — which part of me is. But her reaction was that of the other part of me — that it was normal and understandable under the circumstances — that it is there under any circumstances more than we allow. And that even if it had gone further, it wouldn't be a problem unless I made it that way. I really think that, but somewhere else, I'm fighting awfully hard.

The Process: Saying "The Word"

(1975, January, one week while teaching a
Women's Voice in Modern Literature course)

Monday: *Lesbian* — for two years, more perhaps, I have been unable to write honestly, to write at all. My mind stops there, afraid. I have spoken truthfully to no one. But I may have stopped lying to myself – perhaps. To admit that I do love Sue, that I am physically attracted to many women, would make love to them, do dream of them, have always been more emotionally involved with women – without the ambivalence and fear I feel with a man. I wonder how I seem to the world. I am happier now than I have been for a long time, personally and professionally – many things are good. But things inside me are turbulent, agitated; sometimes I feel like I will crack open from pressure. Having no one to confide in is a problem, but only a small part of it. I have a need to know some things, and no way to inquire. I am relieved to finally be knowing some of this consciously, but it threatens me constantly. (And then I wonder whether it's all in a game I'm playing with myself – a thing I have made up and could just as easily make go away again if I chose. Would I want it to go away? I don't know. Is it real? Or does that matter?)...

Introduced "Women's Voice" today. Talked about the imposed schizophrenia of the woman intellectual. How I always read books about men and identified with men, "knowing" that maleness was the moral, social and cultural norm, but knowing too that I was female. Or thinking I was. But if Molly Bloom was a woman, I must be a mutant. Some of it was getting too close.

Tuesday: Tomorrow is women and madness – how women keep control, how they lose it, what images they use to imagine it – and other enormities. Phyllis says there are also novels of men who are mad, but I don't agree. Portnoy is not mad, just obnoxious. I am furious. Sue is unhappy. Phyllis says it will be better for me when I get away from here. I am mostly content but very lonely: tired and lonely.

Wednesday: Val called today. She wanted to do an independent creative writing project with me. I don't think the department will let me. I'm talking about creating order tomorrow. I don't need that nearly as badly as I need approval and love. Maybe they follow if or when a woman creates her own little ordered enclave? My mind is chaotic, but I'm comfortable with that.

Thursday: I lectured today for one and a half hours. Just once I wish somebody would say, "Wow," or make a connection with this stuff for me. Inappropriate, I guess, since I was talking about the lack of cause-and-effect relationships in women's lives today.

Friday: I'm going through ... Edwin Hawkins Singers. Sue is here. She was at the Van Duyn lecture. I didn't think she'd come up. She sounded sick on the phone. When I first saw her, looking at her, she seemed strange, not familiar, and not attractive – but at dinner all of a sudden there she was again. There. I wonder what she and Lisa say about me. They both know how I feel about Sue. And whenever we embrace I can feel Lisa watching – not jealous even, but very there – observing.

The Process: What It Means

1975, February: Having Blanche Boyd here was important, but more for me than the class. I hadn't planned on letting a radical lesbian have the last word on "Women's Voice." The class responded much better to Linda Pastan, who spoke about trying to put her family and poetry together. People had fewer questions for Blanche. The question I had was personal and I didn't even recognize it until last night. We sat in the kitchen drinking brandy until 4 a.m. talking about god knows what – I can't remember, but it was fantastic. But I never asked my question ... What I want to know from Blanche is: So how did you know? When did you decide you were in fact a lesbian, not bisexual, reacting to a bad marriage, etc. I'm not sure there is an answer, but whenever I have one of my imaginary dialogues with Phyllis, she doesn't believe me and all I have is internal evidence. She probably would believe me, of course. I have this image of announcing to the world (i.e., myself, then Phyllis) that I am a lesbian and having the world pat me on the head, take my pulse, and tell me I'll get over it soon. Obviously I'm not sure yet that I won't. It creates internal tension and I'm afraid if I did talk about it – what? I don't know – afraid it would be real, or it wouldn't? And I'd have to try again with a man.

...So many of my students know I'm vulnerable. Some of them will protect me, others see it as a challenge. Ellen came out to the house tonight. She said Pat was telling other students I had propositioned her. Part of me laughed and part didn't. I told her what had happened, how Pat did this seduction number on me for three weeks and finally I said, "Okay, I want you," and she freaked. I'd never seen her nervous or disconcerted until that moment. It was almost worth the risk. Anyway, Ellen is furious with her.

1975, March: For several days now I've been picking up Jill Johnston's book, *Lesbian Nation,* and reading it when I should have been grading papers. I don't know what I would have thought of it last year, but I think now it is an important political statement. At the same time I doubt my own judgment. Jane said the other day that she doesn't fall in love with people much older or younger than herself — something about experience, etc. I thought that was true for a while, but then I think of Sue. I know I'm afraid of Ellen's promiscuity, not her age — at the same time, I wouldn't mind some casual sex. I ache just to hold another body. I got drunk at Hillary's last night. I was sitting next to her. It's dumb to let myself get so imaginatively caught up where there's no chance of involvement — when others may notice and she could get really pissed off — and I don't have that many other friends.

1975, April: I want a child, but not a man. I want Hillary, but she is with Tom. I'm not sure I ever felt anything about a man. I wish I knew whether I were terrified of sexuality or heterosexuality. I commit myself to men who seem to be able to control me, and then withdraw emotionally. What an incredible thing it is to realize after all these years that I hated dating, that I was never at ease in social situations when I was expected to dance or date or pick up men or whatever. The thing with Dan was typical. I'd really look forward to the ballet or whatever we were going to do, but I never enjoyed spending time with him, even though we had so many interests in common. On paper, he's perfect, I kept telling myself. But I didn't even like him, and I saw him nearly once a week for over a year. I finally went to bed with him just to see if he'd be more interesting. He wasn't — just embarrassing. I can't think of anybody I was ever comfortable "dating." And the men I've lived with became a kind of torture after a while, each in his own way.

The Process: How It Happened

1975, June: I feel more comfortable with my own body and sexuality now than ever before in my life, whether it's negative – knowing that I never have to sleep with a man again – or positive – finding a natural and spontaneous expression of my deepest, most intimate feelings. And I can see sources for this in what I was ten years ago, but this doesn't invalidate that ... I don't even have to reinterpret those events; if Carolyn had kissed me that night in the garden in England, I couldn't have responded positively, even knowing those feelings were there.

When I first started imagining what it might be like to make love with another woman, the idea terrified and excited me. My story line was pretty vague, a lot of embracing and some movement, a little high-fidelity inhalation, but no technicolor and the lens was comfortably out of focus. Usually I was not even a participant.

Fantasies progressed on three different levels as I became more accustomed to the setting. My waking fantasies were the most fun and moved most quickly. Usually in this scenario, a strikingly attractive woman would find me irresistible and allow me to be a passive observer at my own seduction. It seemed an ideal solution at the time – I could learn a few new things without taking the risk of looking foolish or performing badly. I had no access to my sleeping dreams at that time. They were gone before I awoke, like the orgasm I hovered on the edge of but lost with consciousness. The imaginative level I had the most trouble with was the one that came in contact with my everyday life. In all the mundane details of classes and meetings and casual associations, I looked at women with new eyes, but what I was imagining became unimaginable when it was connected with Susan's hands or Carol's hair or Peggy's breasts. I developed a pronounced stammer in certain highly charged emotional situations – like the time in the A&P when I was standing across a grocery cart from Hillary Martin and saw for the first time how incredibly blue her eyes were and felt them looking at the back of my brain.

Meanwhile, my less-conscious fantasies established a pace and direction of their own. From full-blown scenes of faintly developed seduction, I found myself rerunning fragments and details. The projector would run, stick, rewind, run, stick, rewind, ad nauseam, or at least ad emotional fatigue. In one of these scenes, I was standing across from a tall woman with long, blonde hair held back by a barrette. Our eyes would meet in a direct challenge and erotic exchange. I would reach across to her hair, run my hand down the nape of her neck, and unfasten the clasp of the barrette. As her hair fell forward, I would lean to kiss her mouth and the projector would cut off. And cut off again and again.

Finally, my real life began to follow my fantasy life. As I became more comfortable with the idea of loving a woman, I gave myself permission to act on those feelings. I stopped waiting for an aggressive woman to seduce me. I stopped asking women I knew would say no. I stopped worrying about how well I would perform. Last night I took Karen's hand and led her back to my bed. About halfway through the final scenario, I remembered to ask, "Is this all right?"

"Yes," she said with some surprise. "Oh, yes."

Angelus

Testimony

I was forty when I came out to myself. At forty-nine, I came out publicly. It sounds so simple to say, "I came out." But the incremental steps along the way, the feelings and thoughts that allowed me to do that, are very clear and dear to me. The process of coming out can occur by means of little baby steps, long strides, big giant steps, and by great leaps and bounds. I've had experience with all of these.

When I fell deeply in love with a woman at the age of forty during the mid-'70s, I didn't question for even a second that I was a lesbian. My emotional connections had always been with women, and two light affairs spread over the previous twenty years had let me know that sexual relationships with women were exciting. Neither time had I suffered angst over it — I just accepted it as one part of my nature. But suddenly at forty, I knew what all the songs and poetry were about. I was delighted to finally have myself figured out.

It was important for me to discover out lesbians, but even more so to discover black lesbians willing to be out. I wanted more than anything to be able to be completely out in the Connecticut city where I was living then. However, it wasn't safe for me, my business, or my family. During that period, I saw Audre Lorde speak, and heard her siren call: "What are the silences that you swallow day by day?" she asked. "If we wait to speak until we are not afraid, we will be sending messages back from the grave," she said. I knew then that I would live my life as an open lesbian as soon as I was able. I began working to extricate myself from my complicated heterosexual family life so that I could write and speak exactly as I wanted to.

◆

Six years after hearing Lorde's fateful exhortation, I moved to Cambridge to join my lover (not the one I fell in love with at forty). Aside from the desire to live in a politically active community, I was also drawn by the blood family on both sides that my two children could experience. My ex-husband and I were born and raised in Boston, where some of our siblings still lived, which gave my children instant access to relatives, including an eighty-year-old paternal grandmother. Since I never had grandparents, I wanted them to experience her as much as possible while they had the chance. It was a wise decision; she died three years later. That period of time spent nurturing the bond between my children and their grandmother (especially my daughter, who was ten when we moved) was also spent learning to do several things: work for another agency besides my own for the first time in more than twenty years; live as a fairly anonymous member of a community; discover whether writing skills used sparingly for more than a quarter of a century could still work for me.

When I first began writing for the Boston women's newspaper *Equal Times,* anyone reading my first article carefully might have made the assumption that I was a lesbian. It was about Les Ballets Trockadero, a group of male ballet dancers who dressed in tutus and toe shoes and acted female as well as male parts. My ardent plea for eliminating sex roles in ballet might have been a tip-off, if not an outright giveaway. Some of my later pieces for *Bay Windows* and *Sojourner* might also have led one to believe that I was a lesbian. For instance, in one particular *Bay Windows* piece on presidential candidates addressing women's issues, my closing comment was a lament that in listing the various constituencies of women these candidates had to be concerned with, no one had the temerity to bring up lesbians. Of course, all my women's community friends "knew for sure" about me. But I'd never said it publicly or in print. Then in May 1985, the foster care issue hit the gay community.

(In May 1985, Massachusetts governor Michael Dukakis instituted a policy in the Department of Social Services effectively banning lesbians and gay men from being foster parents.)

The Gay and Lesbian Defense Committee held several meetings, which I attended, relating my experience as a lesbian foster mother. As Gay Pride Day approached in June, I was called and asked to speak at the rally on the Boston Common about this experience.

That's when I first realized that I had not been as out as I'd thought, because when I told my life partner that I'd been asked to speak, she expressed fear for me. Somewhat puzzled, I stated that since everybody knew anyway, I didn't know what the problem was. She made me realize that nowhere had I actually stated publicly that I was a lesbian. I was astonished, but it was true. My first flip response was, "Well, then, what better place to do it? Fifteen thousand people can hear it at once, then there certainly can't be any doubt." We discussed for a couple of days the dangers of being out in the larger community versus the relative safety of being a lesbian in the women's community. She expressed her fears for me, for herself, and for the children (a boy who was seventeen at that time, and a girl of eleven). I also took that time to let my children know that this speech was going to happen. It did, and it was a tremendous experience.

The decision to speak to that many people on Boston Common was very scary. But, like Audre Lorde, like Barbara Smith, like Beverly Smith — women I had read and admired during my closet days — I wanted to be out there for that lone black woman who might need to see me at a significant time in her life.

Sometimes we throw ourselves out there and we're never really sure whom we're affecting. But I've had good feedback. One closeted black woman who didn't feel safe enough to come to the rally saw a tape of my gay pride speech on cable. She taped it herself, and then managed to meet up with me later. She said she was so surprised and glad to see my black face that she almost kissed the TV screen. Another closeted woman came to a lesbian workshop I did on Cape Cod as part of a conference by women who had been to the women's conference in Nairobi, and she said she never even imagined that the woman leading the workshop was going to be black. Both these women were as relieved to discover me as I was to discover them, and we have formed ongoing friendships. A relative of mine recently called to say she had just discovered her son is gay and she needed to discuss her feelings and talk about how to handle it. Everything is fine with them now, and I'm delighted I was out there so that she could have someone to turn to.

These are only some of the positive reactions to my being such an out black lesbian. However, lest you think this is an entirely altruistic undertaking, I must say unequivocally that

I'm having absolutely the grandest, most affirming and uplifting time I've ever had. Finally, I feel all together — whole and happy.

My dreams at age forty didn't even begin to prepare me for the freedom I feel at age fifty. So, for anyone shackled in some closet with the door locked, I say, "Keep picking at the lock." No matter how long it may take, you deserve to know this feeling, even if it's for only one day before you die.

This piece and the speech that follows are connected not only in theme but also in feeling, in the manner of "testifying." Taken together, I call them "Testimony."

Gay Pride Speech

June 15, 1985, on Boston Common

Hello. I'm Angela Bowen, a mother and writer, and I'm very happy to be here today. I'd like to tell you a story.

When I was a young married woman with a year-old baby, I moved with my husband to Connecticut to open a dancing school. One day a social worker called to ask if I could find something for a fourteen-year-old girl to do in exchange for dancing lessons. We met, she started baby-sitting for our son, and she eventually began staying late for dinner and on into the evening, obviously hating to return to her foster home at night. When I finally won her confidence, I found out she was being physically abused by the woman, who used to beat her with a broom handle, and sexually abused at night by the 55-year-old man of the house — an elder in his church, by the way. I told the social worker, who asked us to take her into our home. After weeks of persuading a very reluctant husband, and months of looking for a larger apartment so that she could have her own room, I succeeded in gaining a new foster daughter. She lived with us until she was grown, and is now a 35-year-old mother of two. She says I gave her the first respect and sense of family she'd had in years. We're still good friends.

Two years after she came to live with us, my husband's first wife died and his eleven-year-old daughter came to live with us. I legally adopted her, and we raised her until she was grown. She's thirty now, and the mother of a ten-year-old daughter.

I was always the main parent of all the children in our house — but when I took in that foster daughter, I was a new mother with an infant, and I was only twelve and a half years older than the teenager I was raising. But that was okay with the state of Connecticut; they pestered, they called and kept on pressing for the placement while I was trying to convince my husband and looking for a new apartment so the child could have a room of her own. I don't recall any examination, but the social worker was extremely impressed with us: the ideal heterosexual couple with a little baby, and just beginning a business. We'd had no experience with raising children, but — no problem — we'd learn.

The judge who awarded the adoption decree for my step-daughter also thought we were pretty ideal. He especially commented on my strong character. No problem. You see, I was straight, so I had to be okay.

But now, five children later (and after having taught a few thousand as well), if I applied to the Department of Social Services in Massachusetts, I couldn't get a foster child. I'm unfit, says the state. Everything's changed because now I'm aware that I love women. So, all the experience I've gained would mean nothing next to that of a young woman just starting out, as long as she had the shadow of a man beside her, whatever his character, willing or unwilling to open his heart to a child, or lying in wait to assault that child, with his cover of heterosexual respectability saving him from the slightest scrutiny. That's how this homophobic society wastes its resources by throwing us away and wiping out our lives.

What I want to talk about is the potential solidarity this awful incident offers to us all. If some of us have felt alienated from one another, for whatever reasons, all the various factions of the gay and lesbian community can feel solidarity on this one issue, at least, as can all our principled straight friends, families, and political allies.

I can stand up here saying these things because my children are biologically and legally mine, so I'm not in danger of losing them. I also know that whenever sick-minded political opportunists decide to, they can legislate that biological children are endangered by their parents' homosexuality or lesbianism. They won't even need a complainant – just the law. If they come for you tonight and I don't stand with you, they'll be back for me tomorrow. Not one of us is safe, in or out of our closets, until each one of us is legally protected.

We were proud enough to come out today to honor ourselves and our own choices. Some of us barely out, scared, but here. Some stepping a bit more firmly each year, and some of us *waaay* out there. For myself, I've been sticking my head further out each year, but I feel daring and proud today, because I'm speaking for the first time as an openly lesbian woman. Yes, we're gay and we're proud, and I'm so happy for all of us smart enough to have figured out our way past all the obstacles thrown up to prevent us from finding our natural partners in our own particular order of the universe. But let's also be smart enough to get together and *fight*

— not only for ourselves, but for all those children waiting hopefully for loving homes that we've already proved we can provide.

Whatever comes, let's get ready and stay ready. They don't know who they're messing with. Not yet, anyway.

Toni McNaron

My Personal Closet

That first job was the hardest I will ever have. I was
the English department. That meant I taught
three high school classes, in addition to freshman and sophomore courses in the junior-college wing of All Saints. Being a
perfectionist, I believed each student should write a theme a
week. So every weekend for the two years I worked there, I
graded and commented generously on some seventy or eighty
papers. Students found their voices in my classes and went on
to college at some of the "best" schools in the country – all out
of the South at my urging.

My students loved me right away and stayed in my classroom after school to talk about eternal verities and other
similarly unmanageable topics. But they worked hard at reading, memorizing, and writing about literature by all the major
white male authors. As I recall, I did not teach a single female
author. Out of class, we spent idle hours walking in the lovely
woods surrounding the school or shopping in the tiny town of
Vicksburg on Saturday, when they were allowed off campus
without a chaperone. My car was a subject of one of their
many projects. It was a baby blue Volkswagen, the first car I'd
bought on my own. I'd only made one payment before my
arrival. The girls decided it had to have a name and for days

worked on possible options. Finally they settled on "Beatrice Portinari," which combined their fascination with my story about Dante and his ethereal love-muse-idol, and their loose Latin coining of a word to mean "that which carries McNaron," "Portinari." I was moved by their cleverness and their caring.

One of the high school seniors, Mimi, began spending late afternoons talking about music and nature and how much she adored whichever writer we were studying. Mimi was tall and willowy with shiny, silky, dark brown hair that hung down around her shoulders. Her deep-set and bottomless brown eyes looked long and questioningly at me until I was not sure what to do next. She liked French almost as much as English, and gradually I began reading French with her, telling myself I needed to keep up my skill since I was on my way back for more graduate school.

When her teacher assigned Saint-Exupery's *Le Petit Prince* as an extra reading, Mimi jumped at the chance, suggesting that we read it together before compulsory evening chapel. After a day or two of reading at adjacent desks in my classroom, I proposed that we retire to my room on the third floor where we could be more comfortable. Once there, I realized that the only way to be comfortable was to sit on my single bed, since there was only one chair at the small desk provided for letter writing. So tall, willowy Mimi and I began translating a story about a strange and wonderful attachment between a little boy who has fallen from the sky and a fox; a story about taming and being tamed.

Since my dormitory room faced west, our late-afternoon sessions were framed by breathtaking sunsets, which we interrupted our translating to watch. Kneeling on my narrow bed, we'd stare out my little oval window, commenting on colors and rays and the beauty of it all. We tried literally to overlook the cannon on the hill. After one such hiatus, Mimi lay down on my bed instead of sitting back on its edge to continue Saint-Exupery. Seeing the last rays of sunlight had made her drowsy, she said. She napped for the fifteen minutes before chapel, while I sat uneasily in the lone chair watching her. I was aware of feelings I'd never had before, which were periodically erased by waves of fear. What did it mean that I looked so tenderly at this student who clearly trusted me or she wouldn't be napping on my narrow bed in the growing dusk? None of my gay male friends' stories entered my mind as I searched frantically for some familiar mooring on which to pin my strange emotions. It never occurred to me that Mimi might be having similar feelings or even be acting in ways that elicited mine. Since I never asked her about her past, I have no idea where I fit in her sexual history.

At the end of the fifteen minutes, she still slept. I realized I had to awaken her or run the risk of missing chapel and being turned in. Attendance was taken of both students and faculty by the dean of women, Gladyce Cooper. She stationed herself at the back of the church with a clipboard and several alphabetical lists. If a girl missed a second time, she was denied her shopping or dating privileges for three weeks. If she missed three times, her parents were called for consultation preparatory to asking her to leave. If faculty were absent, Gladyce cornered us somewhere inappropriate, like inside a cubicle in the ladies' room. Standing over Mimi as she slept, I broke into a cold sweat. I called to her softly but she seemed not to hear. When I knew that I was going to have to touch her, I gingerly shook her left shoulder with two fingers and saw her eyes open slowly and a shy smile spread over her face. My impulse was either to enfold her in my arms or to run out of the room.

Doing neither, I hurried us off to chapel, where we arrived as Father Allin was saying the Sanctus. Gladyce erased check marks on two pages, and I registered inside that she not only knew we were late but that we were late together. I felt instantly cautious, angry, and protective.

Within a week of her initial nap, Mimi and I had lain down side by side on my single bed. Sleepy from translation, Mimi had once again reclined for the half hour before chapel. Tired myself from a long night of paper grading, I joined her, not consciously suspecting what could so easily happen. Again, Mimi seemed to drift into a sound sleep, while I lay awake, my mind filled with thoughts and my body with new desires, not present when I had slept with two or three men or even when I had felt passion and tenderness for Malcolm. Over the next month, our progress on the bed went from long soulful looks to seemingly innocent hugs to a day when our mouths touched and stayed longer than had been my previous experience. No one had ever seemed to want to kiss me deeply, nor had I wanted them to. I remember my mild discomfort at 1940s movies when Clark Gable and whoever was his current partner filled the silver screen with their French kisses. Their lips seemed too parted, too moist, too hungry, especially his. But when Mimi and I kissed that first time, all I felt was excitement.

Not surprisingly, Mimi and I became lovers shortly after that first kiss. Neither of us felt awkward or shy about how to make love, and neither of us felt guilty about our pleasure. What I cannot remember is what we actually did or how that felt. Sentences I try to write about our frequent meetings either are filled with pulp magazine cliches or read like abstract projections of what two women would do when making love. Though I understand why I cannot bring the sensual details to life, I feel sad and angry. The reason stems from the coincidence of my lovemaking with bimonthly visits to the school director's office. Though I did not let Father Allin's persecution keep me from Mimi, I internalized enough of it to block out the pleasure and satisfaction connected with my first lesbian relationship.

For most of the years between my involvement with Mimi and writing this essay, I felt guilt and shame about our relationship. I saw myself as the initiator of all our activities and felt vaguely dirty for that fact. Finally I am able to understand that Mimi had her part in the process, that she was eighteen and I was twenty-one, though there was a genuine power differential since I was her teacher. But when we became sexual, I distinctly recall that she was not at all surprised or awkward — facts about myself that I've used as signposts of my inherent lesbianism, but which did not function so to define her until recently.

Our initial setting for sexual delights was the logical place: my bed. But not even faculty doors in the dormitory had locks. Mimi and I began to feel anxious and interrupted our delight when we heard or thought we heard footsteps outside or someone turning the door handle. Once, we were barely able to spring up and rearrange our clothing before a student came in to ask me about some poem of Alexander Pope's. She had not bothered to knock, and I felt the same way I had when I saw Gladyce Cooper erase her check marks in chapel: watched, suspected, guilty without quite knowing of what. After that narrow escape, I determined to find a more private, preferably lockable, place for us.

But before I located such a haven, I was called into the rector's office. John Maury Allin was his name, and he later became presiding bishop of the Episcopal Church of America.

That morning in 1958, he tried to preside over my dismissal, but I refused to cooperate. He told me that a student had come to him with a "sickening story" of having seen me the previous evening kissing Mimi in the back of the chapel. My immediate response was "Call her in and have her say that to my face." Maybe I'd read of such scenes in novels and remembered the stoolie's collapsing in the face of the accused. Whatever my model, I was reversing the scene. I was asking the young woman in one of my classes, where I insisted that students name whatever reality they saw in literature, to look me in the face and deny that she'd seen what she had indeed seen. Mimi and I had taken to stealing a good-night kiss in the foyer of the chapel. We'd stay at prayers until everyone was gone and then meet quickly for a few words and some small gesture of endearment.

Father Allin agreed to the meeting, but stipulated that Mimi must be present as well, clearly hoping that she'd give us away. While he sent for the informant, I rushed to the student lounge, which was in a separate building called the Play House. Finding Mimi smoking with her choir friends, I pulled her aside and told her of our plight, that she would have to submit herself to the interview with Father Allin and the as-yet-unknown student. When we all had assembled, it was hard to gauge whose fear and anxiety was the greatest. The student looked at me, burst into tears, and stammered something about being mistaken or exaggerating or mistaking us for someone else. Allin was stymied, which angered him, so that his was the face that reddened. But his only choice was to send us all away.

Since i never spoke to the student who had seen me and my first lover kissing, I have no idea why she took back her story, why she chose in that split second to side with me rather than with the man in authority over us both. The shame I felt at the time, tacitly asking her to lie, I carried with me for many years. Today I am willing to imagine that the young woman simply preferred to help me and Mimi rather than placate a father figure. I had only taught her for a few weeks when the scene took place and do not remember her name. But I owe her my job, since if she had stuck to her story, I would most probably have been forced to leave. Mimi might well have been placed in a difficult position or suspended, though the good rector could have kept her in school by saying that I was the corrupting influence.

Over and over that year, as he continued his accusations, the scenario went something like this: I would get a note from Father Allin, or he'd stop me in the hall as I was returning to class from lunch, or he'd have Gladyce tell me that he wished to see me at such-and-such a time. Steeled against what was to come, I would enter his office and have the door shut firmly behind me. I always waited for him to lock it, since his office did have the capacity for privacy. Usually we were alone, though sometimes Gladyce was there with her ubiquitous clipboard. Twice, we were joined by the dean of academic affairs, Wade Wright Egbert, who not only liked me, but thought me a superb teacher. Father Allin opened each of these grillings with the same phrase: "Toni, I'm going to have to ask you to leave if you don't change your behavior. You're corrupting the young and I can't allow that." His fantasies of what I was doing must have upset him a great deal, because by the end of this brief opener his face would be covered with ugly blotches, making him even more unattractive than he was. He resembled a bulldog, with a very thick neck, tiny eyes too closely set in his face, and fulsome lips that snarled when he spoke. My responses were pretty uniform too, ranging from

"I don't understand what you're talking about," when he was general in his condemnation, to "But you have no evidence so you can't fire me," when he mentioned Mimi specifically. Once when he was particularly vicious, Wade intervened, reminding him of my excellent work with my students, bringing hard evidence in the form of their devotion to literature, their memorization of endless lines by numerous poets, their long cogent papers written and copiously responded to every week. He also reminded his boss that I was the only English teacher they had and it would be impossible to replace me in midyear. Father Allin sputtered and fumed, but backed off for that interview. My gratitude to Wade was expressed in renewed efforts to do my job superbly; my students thrived while I consistently gained weight, drank too much, and slept poorly.

My initial confrontation with Father Allin heightened my sense of urgency about finding a private place for Mimi and me to meet. A place presented itself within the next week. My classroom was across from the library in the basement of the main building. It led, through a narrow corridor, to piano and chorus practice rooms — a fact that gave me pleasure many a night as I sat grading papers. In that corridor were two doors: one to a toilet and the other to some unknown space. Upon looking inside the second door, I found a tiny room full of trash, part of an oil furnace, and a small metal box in which lay a lead key. Our school had a security system comprised of several of these little boxes strategically located on campus. Each evening, an elderly watchman patrolled the grounds, checking in at each watch box by inserting its key into a round clock slung over his shoulder. I never figured out how that activity could possibly alert him to anything amiss, but the watchman was quite faithful.

I decided to make that little room our place, though it had neither lights nor a window. Every night for two weeks, I went directly to my classroom after supper, ostensibly to grade papers. Part of each session was spent filling my two wastebaskets, plus the ones in each empty practice room, with as much trash as I dared without raising the janitor's suspicions. Finally, the room was empty of debris. I cleaned it as best I could, installed a padlock on the inside, gave Mimi the second key, and hoped for the best. What I'd not taken into account was the watchman's schedule of rounds and his need to be able to reach into our room, take out the watch key, and perform his little ritual with the winding clock. We had to delay using our lair until I'd spent another week, ostensibly grading papers, but actually registering the exact time he arrived at that station.

When I felt all was under control, I invited Mimi in for our first evening in privacy. I'd bought flowers, though it was too dark to see them. There, in that literal closet, in constant fear of the curious or fatal knock, my gentle and first lover and I talked and cried and made love. By and large, my scheme worked, though we had narrow escapes. The worst was the appearance of the watchman fifteen minutes before his appointed time. We were lying on our clothes making love; I was experiencing as I always did the sheer luxury of that, compared to our contoured squirming amidst skirts, hose, garter belts, underpanties, and blouses. I recall Mimi's having just laughed softly at something I'd said about her body's resembling a flower — we both referred often to the other in terms right out of the English romantic poets. Suddenly the door was tried, then pushed even harder, as if it were assumed that something had mysteriously gotten wedged against it. I motioned for Mimi to grab her clothes and get behind the door. I threw mine on, talking to the watchman all the while about having bought a lock for the room so that I could have a little hideaway from all the students wanting to sit in my room and talk after hours. By the end of this outlandish tale, I was more or less dressed and I let him in. He pushed open the door, little aware that right behind it stood a stark-naked student who might at any moment break into a sneeze or cough or laugh or uncontrollable cry of sheer terror. His motions with the lead key were reluctant, as if he sensed my lie. But he finished clocking our station, and must have never spoken to the rector about this strange occurrence, or even about my use of the room.

Once he had left the furnace room, I waited to hear the side door open and close, indicating his exit from that part of the building. Then I motioned Mimi from her perch, and we collapsed into tears and laughter. That near-miss happened in March, and I never really relaxed again, though we continued to meet when our schedules allowed. We never spoke of our escape any more than we spoke about any part of our relationship. But the scene of our touching and kissing and of my discovering something new and powerful about myself in a dark hole intended for garbage haunts me. I still prefer not to make love in the dark, and am reluctant to be sexual in anyone else's house. I have felt extreme anger and extreme sadness that my initial lesbian experience was blighted by circumstances, by my own silence, and by a sanctimonious priest on his way to a bishopric. When gay and lesbian organizations urge us "out of the closet," I wince: that phrase has never held a metaphorical significance for me; it only reminds me of the exact locale for the first nine months of my lesbian life.

Lesléa Newman

The Summer of '83

I t was real hot that summer, the summer of 1983. I spent most of my days lying naked on my bed, reading Ann Bannon's Beebo Brinker books. That certainly didn't do anything to cool me down. I had just come out two months before, and I wanted a lover more than I had ever wanted anything in my whole life. I'd been straight for twenty-seven years and I knew there was something wrong the whole time. My mistake was that I thought there was something wrong with me. Why didn't I like being with men? Why would I rather go to the movies, go bowling, go to a natural history museum, go anywhere but to bed with them? I had a problem. I always thought that I was with the wrong man, but the *real* problem was that I was with the wrong sex.

So I moved to Northampton, Massachusetts, in December of 1982, where there were more dykes per city block than anywhere else in the world, or New England at least. Within a few months I was *out* — I cut my hair, threw away my brassieres, bought a pair of Birkenstocks, and moved out of my co-ed cooperative house into an apartment with Anita, a dyke of four or five years. In short, I had done everything but *it,* the big it that I had only read about in every piece of lesbian literature I could find. I felt like a teenager again, when I was the last virgin on the block. When, oh when, would I ever find a lover?

Anita didn't have a lover either that summer, so we spent a lot of time together kvetching, shvitzing, and comparing crushes. One day, after reading a particularly juicy scene from *Odd Girl Out,* I announced to Anita that we had to go dancing that weekend at the Girl's Club, a women's bar a few towns away. Neither of us had ever been there before, and somehow that made it safer and scarier than a dance in our own community. I was determined to go to that bar and bring a woman home with me. After all, it was August already, and if the whole summer passed without me kissing a woman, I knew I would just die.

Anita agreed to go Saturday night. To make things even more exciting, she came up with a bet: whoever was first to ask a woman she didn't know to dance would get her laundry done by the loser for a month. Wow. Stakes were high. I sure didn't want to be shlepping Anita's smelly t-shirts and shorts to the laundromat for a whole month. But just the thought of asking a woman I didn't know to dance made my knees buckle. "Ask someone you don't think is cute," Anita said. "Then it's not such a big risk, and it won't matter so much if she says no." But what good was that? I didn't want to dance with someone I didn't think was cute. And besides, the possibility of someone saying no hadn't even occurred to me. You mean that once I got up my nerve to ask she could refuse? Now I was even more apprehensive.

Saturday night rolled around, and Anita and I spent about two hours trying on everything we owned, before coming up with perfect outfits: she wore light blue jeans and a black muscle shirt; I wore white pants and a red low-cut top. I had bought all kinds of buttons, which we laughingly pinned on each other: SO MANY WOMEN, SO LITTLE NERVE; SOME DO, SOME DON'T, I MIGHT; and START YOUR DAY WITH ME. Of course, as soon as we got to the bar we took the buttons off and hid them in the glove compartment of Anita's car.

The bar was crowded and smoky. To escape the heat, a lot of women were standing around out in the parking lot, including a whole softball team in uniform. I felt really shy walking past all those women who laughed and talked and stood so easily together, some leaning against the parked cars with their hips touching, drinking beers and looking up at the sky. Anita led me inside and we sat down at a little table, listening to the music and watching the women who were dancing. Then we danced together a few times, which was fun, but not exactly what I had come for. *Hell,* I thought, *if I'd wanted to dance with Anita all night, we could have just stayed home and played Michael Jackson records on the stereo.* When a slow song came on, I told Anita I was going to sit at the bar, and she made a motion to follow me. I shook my head. "Anita," I said. "No offense or anything, but if we dance one more dance together, everyone will think we're an old married couple. You go back to our table and I'll go sit at the bar." I looked at my watch. "Let's rendezvous in an hour, okay?" She nodded and left me to meander over to the bar alone.

I sat on a stool with my elbows leaning back on the bar and watched the dancers for a while. A fast song was on now, and I loved watching all those sweaty bodies moving — hips swaying, breasts bouncing up and down, tuchuses shaking. Sigh. I let my glance wander among the tables lining the dance floor, until it landed on a dark-haired woman sitting alone, smoking a cigarette and nursing a beer.

That was *her.* Something in me just knew it. I studied her closely. She was sitting low in her chair, with her arm flung carelessly across the table, and her legs up on the empty chair across from her. She wore a white button-down shirt and tight black pants. No buttons, no jewelry. She was suave, cool, tough, detached. I didn't know the word *butch* yet, but I knew I liked what I saw.

I continued to watch her for a while, wondering just how I would approach such a woman. Soon her head turned slightly and she looked in my direction. My stomach practically fell to my feet, the way it sometimes does when I ride in an elevator, but I held my gaze. A flicker of a smile crossed her face before she turned away. And before I could move she turned back. This time I smiled.

Why had she looked my way? I'd like to think she could feel my stare burning a hole in her cheek, though later Anita pointed out that the clock was hanging on the wall above the bar right behind me. I guess it doesn't really matter why she looked at me. I was just glad she did, which I guess was obvious, because eventually she came over and asked me to dance. I thought for sure she was getting up to leave, or to go to the bathroom or something, but she very slowly and calmly walked up to the bar, stood right in front of me, and said, "Wanna dance?" Just like that.

I nodded and slipped off my stool. She took my hand and led me onto the dance floor. *Oh my God, she'd holding my hand,* I thought as we passed Anita, who was still sitting alone at our table.

We danced two dances together without saying a thing and then what I was dreading and hoping for happened: a slow song came on. She (I still didn't know her name) opened her arms and I gratefully fell into them.

We danced through that song and the next slow one, and let me tell you, she was some dancer. She had both her arms

140

tightly around me and one leg planted firmly between my thighs, rotating in a manner that was driving me wild. And if that wasn't enough, she started planting little kisses down my neck and across my collarbone, which was peeking out of my shirt. I closed my eyes in sheer ecstasy, hoping that Brooke Shields would never stop singing about her "precious love." At one point I looked up and caught sight of Anita still sitting by herself and watching me dance, her eyes practically popping out of her head. I closed my eyes again, letting my body sway and time stand still until the song was over.

After two more fast songs, Mary (I had finally asked her name) asked me if I wanted to get some air. I did, and as we walked out to the parking lot, she took my hand again. I followed her past parked cars with women leaning against them, past some trees, past the lights of the street, toward a darkened corner of a field with a baseball diamond in it. At that point, I would have followed her anywhere. She leaned back against the metal fence and pulled me close to her. *Finally, thank God,* I thought, as her lips met mine. All the reading I'd done, and all the fantasizing, didn't prepare me for the softness and the strength and the rightness of that first kiss. I felt like my whole body was rushing toward my mouth, crying, "More, more!" I got weak in the knees and wet in the pants. My mouth sought hers again and again. "God, you're beautiful," she said, stopping for air, and then pushed her tongue between my teeth once more.

Eventually, we found our way back to the bar, and Anita and I went home. Mary never became my lover − it seems she was nursing a broken heart, and felt it was fine to flirt, but no dessert. And Anita didn't do my laundry for a month either, saying that Mary had asked me to dance, not vice versa, so it didn't count. I maintained that it was my looking at her so hard that brought her over in the first place, so Anita should at least do my laundry for two weeks. But she wouldn't.

That was the highlight of the summer of '83 ... In the car on the way home from the bar, I'd kept asking myself what in the world ever took me so long? I decided I sure had a lot of kissing and hugging and other things to do to make up for lost time. I'm still working on it.

Candyce Rusk

One Sunday

I remember the warm Sunday afternoon distinctly. It was in the mid-'60s — I don't clearly remember the year — but oh, that hot afternoon! I lived in a small midwestern town along the shores of Lake Michigan. Pam, the fifteen-year-old blonde femme fatale of my neighborhood, was with me in my parents' guestroom. I was about thirteen, and all fire and tomboy, hating hair curlers, and playing kick-the-can with the boys.

Pam had big blue eyes, a full toothy smile, and wore her newly developed figure with a definite pride. Kick-the-can didn't interest her, even though she was a fast runner. I was, frankly, on the edge of a strong attraction to her, and very shy.

Shades and curtains drawn, we lay on the divan amidst popcorn and newspapers, eagerly waiting for the world premiere of *The Three Stooges Go to the Moon.* As the opening credits rolled, Pammy turned to me, fluttering her eyes. She placed her newly polished pink fingernails on my thigh. I feigned indifference, though excited by this unusual move. My mind flipped to Annette Funicello, the cutest and best-developed Mousketeer. I had a strange feeling about Annette — a feeling I know now as attraction, and, well, adolescent lust. But here was Pam, her fingers running down my leg, slowly.

She turned. "If you had to be a Stooge, which one would you be?" Her voice chimed in my head.

"Oh, Moe," I answered quickly. "He doesn't get hit as much and he's the big shot."

"Really now, Moe, that hair," she replied. "At least yours is blonde." Her arm smoothly encircled my shoulder. Moving slow as molasses, her fingers moved up my neck.

As the Stooges raced around on the screen, my young heart thudded loudly in my chest. I closed my eyes and hoped my brothers and sister wouldn't barge in.

"Where's the newspaper?" Pam asked, suddenly moving away. She grabbed the paper off the floor, her madras pants pulling tight and revealing her smooth upper backside. I thought briefly of temptation and sin, being a Catholic, and then pushed it from my mind.

"See this?" Pam's long finger was fixed on a movie ad from a James Bond film. A seminude model was reclining seductively on a couch, her head close to the floor, her breasts on the edge, pointing majestically upward.

"Yes, I see it," I said gruffly. "What about it?"

"She's beautiful, don't you think?" questioned Pam.

"Sure," I answered, struggling to remain cool. What was she getting at, anyway? According to the nuns at school, anybody who saw a James Bond film was a "pagan." Pam was a Lutheran and obviously going to Hell, unless I could convert her to the Catholic Church. Given the way things were progressing, that seemed highly unlikely.

"Let's play James Bond." She faced me fully, her chest heaving with excitement. "You ... you be James Bond, and I'll be her — the girlfriend." She reached gently for my glasses and slid them under the divan. The world went soft around the edges. Squinting, I watched as Pam's arms crossed in front of her. She pulled off her sweater. Such a rib cage! And her bra! All lace. I'd only seen bras like that on the mannequins at Penny's Department Store downtown. Certainly I didn't own one. I was glad she was playing the girlfriend —she was so well equipped for the part.

"Now..." She got up and opened a closet door. "A gown, or a robe." Pam pulled out a gaudy black negligee someone had given my mother as a joke. She put it on. The top half of Pam was all woman. The bottom had pants which stuck out merrier than twin plaid Christmas trees. Still, I was duly impressed.

"All right." She moved, standing directly in front of me. "You go into the closet and act like you just came back from a spy mission." Getting up, I gave her a wide-eyed look, fully aware that this was far more serious than our usual pretend games.

Once inside, I heard the muffles from the Three Stooges soundtrack. Pam was positioning herself with great pains on the couch, judging from the sound of things. I felt silly and flushed in the dark closet. A strong pulsing of blood wound its way through my body. Would Pam want me to kiss her? I didn't have any practice, except when I kissed my own wrist.

Finally she called me out, "All right, James ... Mr. Bond ... come in, please." I filled my chest with air, simulating a burly strength. I wouldn't find out till years later that Bond was suave and slim.

I strode out of the closet, surprised and deeply delighted at Pam's invitation. Her gown was open, her breasts pointing majestically upward. I froze, unsure.

"On top of me," Pam breathed, air stuck in her throat. I lay on top of her ... just like that. Pam's upside-down face was turning red. "Come *on,* dummy." I responded to that request. I lay down on her, feeling her warm curves and bones. My

145

face was in line with her breasts. Pam sighed. I thought I was squishing her.

"Now kiss them." Plural. That meant two. That meant her breasts. Oh my God. I bent down, my lips nuzzling along the edges of her lace bra. I was aware of their soft sponginess. "Now pull it down," Pam urged. I tugged gently and her breasts jiggled, waiting to be set free. Sympathetically, Pam pulled her bra up. I stared at her nipples, such a light soft pink. I felt them looking at me. "Kiss them." I kissed. So soft. So warm. So Pam. "Now circle them with your finger." Slowly I outlined her breasts, shuddering, truly amazed at the sensuality of this game. My own breasts were tingling, as was the lower half of my body. I wanted her hand there, touching me. Pam moaned and we melted into each other.

From out of nowhere, my little brother shouted, "Hey, open up, you guys!" I guiltily slid off of Pam, sideways. She fell to the floor, her bare half disappearing from me. "I wanna watch the movie, you TV hogs!" my sibling screamed from the far side of the world. Pam, flushed and insulted, hissed at me, "James Bond doesn't have any brothers!" She quickly adjusted her bra, and removed herself from my mother's nightgown. As she grabbed for her sweater, my heart sank. I realized I had crossed some border and was forever changed. I'd had a confusing but sweet glimpse at sensuality, the gentle give-and-take of desire.

Later that night, the sultry day became evening and the sun turned a deep red. Pam and I rode our bikes to the Dairy Queen on Main Street. I insisted on buying her a cherry-coated vanilla cone, perhaps because it reminded me of her soft, soft breasts.

I didn't know that Pam would turn quickly to boys after our encounter, excitedly relating to me stories of her sexual progressions. I stayed spinning in a state of desire for her, ready and waiting for another cue that never came.

Years later, when both of us were in college, I visited Pam at her apartment for the weekend. As we lay together on a double mattress on the floor, she turned to me. "Ever make it with another girl?" she asked offhandedly. It dawned on me that the rite of passion we had shared was buried somewhere in her subconscious. "I've fooled around a bit," I sighed, "but I guess it wasn't serious." We turned from each other then, our sharing forever sealed. Listening to a Buffalo Springfield album, my mind wandered back to the old neighborhood. Hard rocket baseballs, kick-the-can, the Three Stooges, the Beatles. How many people can associate an erotic memory with the Three Stooges? I can — that warm Sunday afternoon with Pam.

Liz O'Lexa

You Must Not Be Doing It Right

Coming out is not a singular, one-time event. Whenever we step from being another face in the crowd
toward being an individual who has a name and a personality,
we're again faced with the decision of coming out. And again
and again, as long as we continue to have the defiance to exist.
We don't all dye a purple streak down the middle of our hair,
quit our job, start a "womyn"-owned business, and secede
from the patriarchy by embracing lesbian separatism, although
I know one dyke who did.

The beginning of my journey was coming out to myself. It
happened in 1975, when I was fourteen and my knee touched
the knee of the most beautiful woman in my Minneapolis high
school, Julia, and I felt an undeniable surge of sexual excitement. All of my life experiences seemed to come together at
once, and I knew I'd discovered the core of myself. I finally
saw all that I'd been feeling in a new, sexual light, and I found
the word for myself: *lesbian*.

I could go on endlessly about Julia, how much this first love
meant to me, how I wanted to spend the rest of my life with
her, how she was intelligent, athletic, absolutely beautiful, and
completely unattainable. My first love never became anything

more than a sweet fantasy that filled my mind throughout high school. Once, I kissed her on the cheek — a terribly brave gesture, because social kissing, even at Christmas, was something that took place in another world.

Years later, I wondered why I was so frightened of telling her how I felt. I thought for a while that it was racism, since she was black and I was white and our worlds outside the classroom were strictly segregated. I'm honest enough to admit that might have been part of the reason, but most of it was that I was afraid. I was lonely and refused to risk having the one and only fantasy that kept me company pulled out from under me.

Just before we started college, I did come out to her. But I didn't have the guts to tell her then that I loved *her,* Julia, the woman who was still to me the most beautiful, gentle, desirable woman on earth, and who'd also become deeply entrenched in the "cool" crowd, smoking weed and sleeping with men. Seven years after our knees first touched, I ran into her on a bus, and at the end of a long ride I told her that she was my first love. We bravely hugged each other during the middle of rush hour in a rather rough section of downtown.

The very first time I actually told anyone — the first time I ever said the word *lesbian* out loud — was completely unplanned. I was seventeen, in my senior year, and I'd landed an incredible job as one of the editors of a student-operated tabloid newspaper. We were the crème de la crème of up-and-coming high school journalists pulled predominantly from the best schools.

We — six other student editors and our very hip adult editor in chief and I — were in the midst of a pre-brainstorm session lunch. I was seated across the table from a man who was to become a longtime friend (and would later come out

---

149

himself) retelling a stunt pulled at school: someone had pasted a "Kiss Me I'm Gay" sign on someone else's back. Our very liberal editor in chief said rather quietly but firmly, "We don't think those kind of jokes are funny because one of our staff is gay."

I just about crawled under the table. *How did she know about me?* Then, as my internal panic subsided, I realized: *There must be someone else who's gay! I'm not the only one!*

I looked cautiously at each person at the table and placed my bet on a thin, short-haired, rather butch-looking woman, our photographic editor. Later, I found out that I was wrong; Katie was from an avant-garde family and was just a couple of years ahead of the androgynous look. The point is, I *had* to know who it was, and since I couldn't be sure by guessing, the only way I thought I could find out was by revealing myself.

In the car on the way back to the office, I told our editor in chief that I was a lesbian. She nearly drove the car onto the curb and gave me the most unequivocally positive response I've ever gotten, particularly when she found out that it was the first time I'd told anyone.

When we reached the office, she introduced me to David, the other gay person on the staff. He later introduced me to gay theater in Minneapolis and long soul-searching talks unlike any I had had before. The editor assured me that everyone on staff was tolerant, if not supportive, and I decided to make an announcement to get my coming out off on the right track. Impulsively, I stood on a chair to announce my lesbianism, an honesty equaled only by marching in the New York pride day parade. After our meeting was over, as we were leaving the building with the sun setting dramatically, David bid me farewell by proclaiming, "Welcome out!" It was an extremely positive, unusual, and good start.

Like a snowball rolling down a mountain, I kept coming out to the important people in my life. During one of our soul-searching talks on the telephone, David convinced me that I should tell my parents. He planned on telling his, and he knew his mother, who loved him very much, would take it well. Besides, being closeted to your own parents smacks of dishonesty that shouldn't exist in a good parent-child relationship.

In another bravado gesture, I asked David to hold the phone. I walked into the living room, where my parents were watching *Charlie's Angels,* turned down the sound on the TV and said, "Mom, Dad, I have to tell you something. I'm a lesbian."

My father replied, "Bullshit. Turn the sound back up."

I told them that I knew it was difficult for them to accept and asked them to think about it for a while, and that I'd talk about it later. Then I hightailed it back to the phone and the safety of my room. Talking to David then gave me the courage to go back out and face my parents twenty minutes later.

Mom, Dad, and I talked for a long time, and we cried a little, too. But they eventually reaffirmed what I'd always known: that they love me very deeply and will always be my staunchest supporters. After much pleading and cajoling three years later, they marched in my first gay pride parade with me, carrying a sign that said, "WE LOVE OUR LESBIAN DAUGH-TER." Appropriately, that year, 1981, the theme of the parade was "Love in Action." Later, Mom said she had no regrets about it — except that it took three days for her girdle to dry out.

Since I had all this unbelievable support, one would expect me to be unrealistically happy, but I wasn't. I was out to myself, my co-workers, and my parents, but I had yet to actually have a relationship with another woman. I was still incredibly lonely, and wanted to become a part of the city's lesbian community. At first it didn't seem necessary to come out into the lesbian community, but in reality it was. I had to assert myself and find a place to fit in.

There were no lesbian bars in Minneapolis, and there was one women's bar in St. Paul, but it was out of the question, since it was more than two hours away by bus. There was, however, an alcohol-free space called the Women's Coffee-house. After discovering it, it took me about a year to find the nerve to go there. In the meantime, I found the Amazon Bookstore, my refuge from the overwhelmingly straight world. It supplied me with tons of reading materials and lesbian-positive images, but it was hardly a social nucleus for me.

My experience in "the lesbian community" got progressively more negative, because everyone, myself included, was uncomfortable with my young age. When I did make it to the Women's Coffeehouse, I was shunned, because I was a stranger. Everyone was already quite well organized into cliques. I searched on until I discovered a building called the Lesbian Resource Center, and I joined the coming-out group. I thought it wasn't appropriate, since I was already out, but it was a way to meet other lesbians. Unfortunately, the friendships didn't last too long. As a first-year college student, I had little in common with women concerned about their careers, house buying, and their long-term relationships with lovers.

I tried fitting into the "politically correct" community. I joined the brand-new *Lesbian Inciter* newspaper collective. At the meetings, I was confronted with the process of consensus, the ideals of separatism, more ageism, and the politics of class.

But I was still very much on the outside, and *lonely*. After meetings, the women broke up into cliques and ignored me.

At that point, it would have been more meaningful if someone had asked me if I'd had a nice day than about my experience in the patriarchal university. But no one ever asked me if I'd had a nice day or how my classes were.

Then I joined a small single-lesbians' group, which was composed of the few *Lesbian Inciter* women who weren't in monogamous couples, none of them under forty. Most of them were into discussing their unfulfilling, short-lived relationships. And there I was, still looking for my first one! I made the decision to leave that group the night one woman said she didn't masturbate because it just wasn't as good, wasn't as "fulfilling" as having a partner. Speaking as one who'd done nothing but, during the break I put my arm around her and whispered, "Diane, about masturbation: you must not be doing it right."

Years later, I heard about something called "internalized homophobia," which is learning to hate yourself and distrust those around you because society hates you. Phobias are fears. Straight people who fear queers are dangerous enough, but when we begin to fear each other and consequently ourselves, then we create a divided community open to only a select few. Homophobia makes "them" want to lock us away from "them," but it also makes *us* want to lock *us* away from ourselves and each other.

I consider myself lucky. I am supported and loved by the many important people in my life, friends and family, and in retrospect, I can almost understand why I wasn't welcomed with open arms into a community where I felt I belonged. Ultimately, I did have my first sexual experience, and have even had a couple of monogamous relationships. I moved to Baltimore, where I'm currently living, and found a "new" lesbian community completely different from that of Minneapolis. I've heard that the Minneapolis community is much changed now, and includes dykes even younger than I was.

Ironically, Minneapolis does seem friendlier now that I'm living in Baltimore. It could be because the lesbian community has changed, or because as I age I become more comfortable with myself. Or it could have something to do with my last visit, when I seduced one of the most beautiful women in the Twin Cities area. Most likely, it's because I'm learning that there is no "right" or "wrong" to coming out. My lesbianism is an integral part of my individuality, and each time I assert myself I come out, sooner or later. My coming-out story is my life story, which is harder to end than it was to begin. Since coming out is a lifelong process, there's always the possibility of a new beginning.

Nancy Wechsler

Front-Page News

The most recent wave of the gay liberation movement, while not responsible for anything as dramatic as saving my life, is responsible for my sanity. I went to public school in Levittown, New York, when girls were to be girls, and boys were to be boys. It was a time when dresses or skirts were mandatory, when girls were supposed to care about how they looked, and care about what boys thought of them. I fudged it through elementary school by wearing pants under my skirts — but if by sixth grade that was getting a bit tough, by seventh grade there was no way I could pull it off. I settled for changing right after school, into more comfortable clothes I kept in my gym locker.

As soon as I learned to talk and walk, I engaged my parents in constant battles over what I was willing to wear and how I would or would not behave. In a world where girls were feminine and less athletic than the boys, I was as good at most sports as any of the boys in my neighborhood. I walked tough, played rough, and engaged in spitting competitions with my neighbors.

While part of me thought I might grow up and get married, I wondered how I would ever survive in a world where women wore dresses and makeup. Would I go through some magical transformation? As the years went by, I realized no such transformation was taking place. I pictured myself growing up to be the only woman who wore pants all her life. Though I could not imagine giving in to societal pressures, neither could I project the shape my life would take.

Those early pre–women's liberation, pre–gay liberation days were difficult. Feeling alone, isolated, ugly, and an outcast with other outcasts as my friends for all those years took its toll. Not a day passed during which I was not harassed as I walked to school or to the store. Catcalls and chants of "Are you a boy or a girl?" hounded me constantly.

While I "felt up" another girl in the backseat of our family car, and pined away over movie actresses (Julie Christie and Geraldine Chaplin particularly caught my eye in *Dr. Zhivago*), it didn't occur to me that I was a lesbian. I think my mother had her fears, but never mentioned them to me until I brought it up years later. In the pre-Stonewall days of my elementary and secondary school years, I'm not sure I knew lesbians existed. In high school, I discussed Camus, Kafka, Shakespeare, the Vietnam War, and the civil rights movement with my close friends, many of whom also came out years later, but we didn't manage to help each other realize we were queer. We lacked the necessary information about sex, and lived in a community that would not have enthusiastically received news of our desires. Mostly, we suppressed our sexual desires. I channeled mine into athletics, while my friends devoted themselves to drama club, orchestra, or schoolwork.

My greatest joys as a youngster revolved around sports. I was very lucky that our junior and senior high school had comprehensive women's sports programs. I played on almost every girls' varsity team: tennis, basketball, volleyball, softball, and field hockey. I became good friends with my gym teacher, who taught me to ski, and along with my math teacher and a group of five or six boys, we all went together on weekend ski trips to New England.

But still, with all the joys and recognition that athletics brought me, I could not shake the feeling that something was wrong with me. I had grown up listening to my mother expound on the wonders of sex, about how it was one of the most beautiful things in the world. When at an early age I asked her about masturbation, she smiled and told me, "Oh, everyone does that, it's fine." In such a liberated family, what was my problem? I could not imagine feeling the joy of sexual excitement my mother described. When I finally did sleep with some men, it was at best boring, at worst physically painful. My mother's words rang in my ears as I lay on my back — dry, in pain, wishing it were over. The year I slept with men was the only time in my life that I got up and out of bed early in the morning — anything to limit the possibility of having more sex. No relationship lasted more than two or three months.

In September 1970, I picked up a book called *Sisterhood Is Powerful,* edited by Robin Morgan. Although it contained very little lesbian content, it didn't really take much to open my eyes to the fact that I was a lesbian. I sought out all other literature of the early women's and gay movements, including *Women-Identified-Women,* a pamphlet by Radicalesbians, and joined a consciousness-raising group. Finally, I felt part of a larger movement that was challenging the sex-role stereotyping and confinement that had plagued me.

I don't remember hearing about the Stonewall Rebellion in 1969, but I do remember the very beginnings of gay activism in Ann Arbor, Michigan, where I was attending college. An out lesbian ran for student government on a slate with several radicals. A chapter of the Gay Liberation Front (GLF) was formed, and later some lesbians split to form Radicalesbians (RL). A few years after that GAWK — the Gay Awareness Women's Kollective — was formed and I joined. GAWK organized consciousness-raising groups, did public outreach and educationals around being a lesbian, and participated in demonstrations. In the early '70s, Ann Arbor had a very organized left, a small but active gay liberation movement, and a strong but disorganized feminist movement. There were CR groups, women's caucuses of groups like the Ann Arbor Tenants Union, and other left groups, and a women's newspaper. I was involved in many of these activities and remember that in addition to talking about the sexism within mixed left organizations, we worked on issues such as day care, abortion, and other reproductive rights. While there was a sense of being involved in the beginnings of a movement, it was a movement without the structure and culture of what we might today loosely term our community. I remember the night a member of our lesbian CR group told us that she had an incredible record to play for us ... and she put on the first album of lesbian music, *Lavender Jane Loves Women* by Alex Dobkin and Kay Gardner. Lesbian novels were few and hard to come by. A friend loaned me her incredible collection of lesbian trash from the '50s. The university established offices of gay and lesbian concerns and women's concerns, and they served as drop-in centers.

In those early years, I didn't experience the clash many feminists experience between the left and the gay or women's movement. It was actually through the socialist group I belonged to that I first met openly gay people and attended gay liberation demonstrations. My leftist friends from that time, many of whom are still friends and are politically active today, immediately chose to join in and support the rebelliousness and spunkiness of the gay movement. We all believed that challenging societal norms was what both the New Left and the gay movement were about.

While I knew some members of CLP and RL, I was rooted in the left, where most of my friends were straight. One year, I lived with nine of my cohorts from the Ann Arbor Tenants Union. I told some of them I thought I was a lesbian. They were supportive, but since they were straight, it didn't give me the chance to explore or take action regarding the part of me that was beginning to think I was queer. I wrote in my journal over and over, "I am a lesbian, I am a lesbian, I am a lesbian," hoping it would sink in and become comprehensible. Then I tore it to shreds and threw it out. It was 1970 and I was scared. My worst fear was that maybe I wasn't really a lesbian. Maybe sex with women wouldn't feel good either; maybe I was frigid, doomed to an existence devoid of the wondrous sexual energy my mother had taught me about. My fear kept me locked inside myself for three years, until in 1973 I was dragged out by a friend who not only took me to lesbian parties and introduced me around, but gave me my first passionate kiss.

In 1971, I graduated from the University of Michigan. I became coordinator of the city's Human Rights–Radical Independent Party (HRP), a third party that had begun the year before with the merger of several radical socialist student groups. While originally skeptical of the idea of socialists participating in electoral politics, even third-party politics, I became convinced that this was an important area to work within. With the slowing down of the Vietnam War, and the subsequent slowing down of the student movement, HRP gave the Ann Arbor left a chance to reach out beyond the student community with a broad platform for social change. HRP was as committed to organizing and participating in demonstrations and strikes as it was committed to running in city, county, and school board elections. Having a radical third party that ran against Democrats and Republicans alike allowed us the opportunity to educate people about the similarities between the two major parties, and particularly about the historical role of the Democratic Party in co-opting and diffusing mass movements for social change.

In 1972, still pondering the question of whether or not I was a lesbian, I was urged to run for city council from Ward 2, where HRP felt fairly confident it could win. I had spent a good deal of time trying to find other candidates, as I lacked the self-confidence to run. Noticing that men in the party seemed not to have that problem, I began thinking of running to challenge my own socialization as a woman.

I had many qualms, fears, and questions about running for office. In addition to my insecurities, I wondered how it would change my life. Among my many qualms about running was the fact that I thought I was a lesbian, but I hadn't yet slept with a woman. Only my good friends in the party knew I thought I was queer. Did this mean I had to get up in front of three or four hundred people at our nominating convention and say, "Look, there is something you might want to know before you nominate me. I might be a dyke"? I wasn't ready to make that statement. I talked it over with other HRP activists, my friends and housemates, and finally went to talk to my friends in GLF for support and advice. I told them that if they believed I should get up at our meeting and say I was gay, I would. Was I gay if I hadn't yet even slept with a woman? Would running as an openly gay candidate be truthful? CLP's response was supportive and nonjudgemental.

They told me, "Look, you don't know if you are gay or not, you don't have to come out. We know you support us, and that you've been at every gay demonstration and every picket line. We trust you. You'd have a better chance to get elected if you didn't come out, and we'd like you to get elected."

Looking back, I feel mixed about their advice. Perhaps I needed someone to help me work through my questions so that I would be able to come out, even though I hadn't yet had lesbian sex. I am sure the party would have nominated me either way. But as I am writing this, over ten years later, I realize that I can't really fault GLF for not being able to do for me what I was not ready to do for myself. So while I did not announce in front of all HRP that I thought I was queer, I did make a promise to myself that every time I spoke, every debate, every talk show, every door-to-door canvas, I would mention the gay liberation part of our platform. That was a promise I kept, and so in looking back on my campaign I feel no shame.

GLF was supportive during the entire campaign, and during my two years on the city council. It was during our first year on the council, before either of us were publicly out, that Jerry DeGrieck (HRP–1st Ward) and I introduced and got passed an HRP-written amendment to the city's human rights ordinance banning discrimination based on sexual preference.

When we came out publicly — at a council meeting during our second year — it was front-page news. We took the occasion of a visit to the council by the chief of police to question him about the lack of enforcement of the human rights ordinance, and his failure to educate his officers about the ordinance. The amount of hate mail that Jerry and I regularly received jumped, and mine was now filled with epithets against my being a Jew, a commie, *and* a queer — an obviously unacceptable condition to some of the people of Ann Arbor and surrounding communities.

Despite the hate mail, I experienced coming out publicly as exhilarating and liberating. It literally gave me the energy to finish my second year on the council even though I was also dealing with my mother's slow death from cancer. A new period had begun for me of intense crushes, passionate sex, wonderful beginnings, and difficult breakups. I learned about what turned me on and who turned me on. I was like an adolescent, and I had a lot of catching up to do. I walked around Ann Arbor with a high I had never experienced before or since — I had finally found and accepted myself, and I had found and become a part of a gay and lesbian community.

Having two openly queer radicals on the city council made for some lively times. GLF and HRP (which was by this time approximately one-third gay and lesbian) organized demonstrations which closed down city council meetings as we demanded public space, recognition, and an understanding of our politics. Far from the respectable image some gay politicians today would like us all to have, we raised hell and did not try to pretend we were the same as everyone else.

My experience of being so openly gay in Ann Arbor affected choices I made later on when I moved to Boston in 1974. Taking a job in a social service agency in Somerville, I was discouraged from coming out by all those around me. But coming out at work, in political groups, and in my neighborhood was important to me, as well as being important politically. Closets provide only a false sense of safety. Coming out is still one of the most important acts a gay person can make. I've always urged my friends to push the limits of what they think might be possible, to give some serious thought to coming out at work, at school, and to their family.

I got involved in the gay and lesbian liberation movement not because of some altruistic notion that it would make a better world, and not simply because I had an analysis which confirmed that gay and lesbian liberation was a threat to the nuclear family, and, therefore, to capitalism. I got involved because it was what was needed to make a world in which I could live and grow, and so that things would be better for those who came after me. I did not "come out in the women's movement." I have always been a lesbian. But it was the women's and the gay and lesbian liberation movements which gave me a name for what I was.

The women's movement and the gay and lesbian liberation movement also allowed me some space outside the confines of my sex role. Since it is these broader politics which engaged me to begin with — not simply a desire for "gay rights" — it is these politics which feed and nourish me now. And with the re-emergence in the '80s of strong pressures once again to conform to feminine stereotypes, it is these broader politics of gay and lesbian liberation and their challenge to the norms of the dominant culture, the nuclear family, "normal sexuality," and traditional gender roles that we so desperately need to articulate now.

Lynn Kanter

Overlooking the Obvious

When I was a young child in the 1950s, I thought that women and men always wore formal attire when they went out on a date, and that the man routinely carried the woman in his arms. The image I had was quite clear: the woman in a swirly silver gown and matching high-heels, the man in a black tuxedo and white shirt, effortlessly lifting his date to spare her such mundane chores as walking from the car to the door.

I didn't understand that a "date" had anything to do with sex or romance. I didn't realize that a wide range of apparel was permissible. I only knew that I did not want to wear a swirly silver evening gown and be carried in some man's arms.

By the time I became a teenager and went out with boys myself, I had, of course, given up this strange concept of dating. But in that predawn of feminism, there were conventions more difficult to buck. One was the expectation that girls were to instantly discard the plans we had made with each other if the slightest chance arose to spend time with a boy — any boy. I could never get over the fact that this behavior was not only considered acceptable, but strongly encouraged. My inclination was exactly the opposite.

In fact, my inclination was the opposite of the norm in any number of ways. All my silver-screen crushes were on actresses. I developed intense attachments to my female friends. On streets and buses, I noticed only the women. My favorite movie was *The Children's Hour*.

You might think all of these idiosyncrasies would serve as clues to my true nature. But to think that would be to disregard my lifelong talent for overlooking the obvious.

♦

Her name was Amy. She lived one floor above me in the dorm of a women's college in upstate New York. Amy had blue eyes, small hands, long blonde hair. She was twenty-one, an age that at nineteen I considered alluringly mature. She had lived her entire life in one tiny town, an achievement to someone like me, who had spent my teens moving with my family from state to state. She was bright, observant, energetic. Best of all, she was a marvelous storyteller.

Amy's life was full of small adventures, and she recounted each one with such color, verve, and freshness that the story seemed to unfold right there in her overfurnished dorm room. She acted out all the parts, creating vivid characters with the tiniest of details – the hitch of a shoulder, the tilt of a head, the flawless replication of an accent.

I found Amy endlessly entertaining, and started spending most of my evenings with her. At about ten o'clock, after I had finished studying, I would bolt upstairs to be greeted with a cup of thick, sugary coffee that Amy had made on her forbidden hotplate. We would tell each other stories and share the day's experiences, joined occasionally by friends drawn in by our laughter. Eventually the friends would drift, yawning, away, but Amy and I would chatter on, stopping only when interrupted by the cacophony of morning birds. Entire nights vanished without a trace. This happened over and over again.

I described the mystery of the disappearing nights to my friend Charlotte, a woman with the sallow skin, jutting jaw, and darkened teeth of advanced anorexia. Sitting up weakly in her bed, surrounded by pillows that could not protect her from her own sharp bones, Charlotte smiled knowingly and said, "Looks like you're on to something new."

I did not ask her what she meant, just as I didn't ask her why she couldn't eat or how serious her illness was. Her eyes closed wearily. After a few moments, I turned out the light, closing her door softly behind me. Charlotte left school soon after that. I never saw her again.

Meanwhile, other mysteries were taking place in my life, mysteries I didn't share with my friends. I appeared to have lost both my ability and my need to sleep. Everything began to fascinate me: classes, cookware, a new book, a song I had heard hundreds of times before. My energy was inexhaustible, fueled by the nightly narrative marathons in Amy's room. And most baffling of all, my hormones appeared to be in an uproar. A sexual current was running through me all the time for no apparent reason.

Very late one night, I set my empty cup on Amy's cluttered dresser and looked around for my shoes. "I'd better go," I told her, "before those damned birds start singing again."

"Why don't you stay?" she asked. "It's too late for you to be walking downstairs to your room."

I hesitated. This seemed plausible, though the commute would have taken about thirty seconds.

"Come on." Amy patted a spot beside her on the bed. "I won't touch you."

Of course *she won't touch me,* I thought as I removed my jeans but primly retained my t-shirt and underwear. What made her think I was worried about that? Why would she even say such a thing? Gingerly I lay down with my back toward her, teetering on the edge of her narrow dormitory cot.

Amy lied. She did touch me, and I touched her, all through what remained of the night. We didn't put a name to what we were doing; we didn't even acknowledge we were doing it. But we were making love, and it was the most thrilling experience I had ever known.

Seconds later, it seemed, the sun broke through the window blinds. Outside our door, rubber soles slapped down the hall toward the bathroom. Amy and I kissed good-bye, with barely enough time to shower and change for class.

I remember with perfect clarity the exultation that lifted me on that spring morning two decades ago, and the thought that sounded in my head as I floated down the stairs to my own room: *Thank God I'm not normal.*

What I meant was: Thank God I don't have to be ordinary. What I meant was: Thank God I'm safe from the staid suburban life for which I've been trained all these years. What I meant was: Thank God I finally know where I belong, and it's in a woman's arms.

I had almost – but not quite – come out to myself. In the easy, earnest ethos of the times, I believed that I was now free to love wherever my heart led me, whether that meant men or women. I did not yet think of myself as a lesbian.

The school I attended, Kirkland College, had been born in the 1960s and died in the '70s, shortly after I graduated. It was remarkable in many ways, one of them being that it was considered unremarkable for women to love women. Rita Mae Brown came to speak, and Alix Dobkin played a women-only concert in the student coffeehouse. I remember seeking advice from my favorite professor about whether I should stay with a man I was dating or drop him in favor of the woman I was also seeing. We had this debate in front of the man himself, by discussing an analogous passage in *Howard's End*.

So not until I left college and reached the "real world" of Chicago, where feminism was blowing through the city like the raw, powerful wind off the lake, did I realize that following my flighty heart was no longer enough. I had to face the fact that it was no coincidence that the people I fell in love with were women. I had to claim the name *lesbian,* with all the pride, power, and defiance that word implies. I had to choose sides. And when I did — swiftly, and with the gratitude of having found a home at last — *that* was my coming-out experience.

Or at least it was one of them. Like most lesbians, I've had many more.

There was the first time I came out to a friend, hesitantly doling out my words on the dark back porch of her parents' house, as Joni Mitchell's "Little Green" quavered from the radio. Sarah listened to me with perfect openness and generosity throughout that tumultuous summer. It was the season of Watergate, the month Richard Nixon resigned from office, but I was too distraught over the dissolution of my relationship with Amy to pay attention to the dissolution of our government. Years later, I would let Sarah drift out of my life because she chose a way of life I could not accept, marrying into Orthodox Judaism with its disrespect for women.

There was the time I came out to my parents, weighing the possibility that I might lose them against the certainty that I would lose them if I kept my true self a secret.

There was the time I came out to my grandmother, who told me she had known for years and wasn't it nice I had found such a lovely girl.

There was the time I came out to a friend from high school, a straight woman who agreed that the teenage intensity we had once felt for each other must have been love.

There was the time I told my boss, and the time I insisted she tell a job candidate she was interviewing so we'd have no homophobes in our department, and the time when National Coming-Out Day rolled around and I couldn't think of another soul to tell.

Then there are the times I've forgotten to come out. My aunt was recently shocked to learn that I had broken up with my partner of ten years – shocked because she hadn't realized that we were together. She had seen my partner at innumerable family events; she had been in our home with its two female occupants and its single bedroom. At what point should I have taken my aunt aside and said, "By the way, you *do* realize I'm a lesbian"? And yet, by mentioning my separation, I was not coming out; I was merely behaving like a person who believes her life's events are worthy of inclusion in the family tapestry.

Even now, after these years of practice, coming out is not always easy. I surprise myself sometimes by stumbling over the words; occasionally I substitute the word *gay* for the more proud and precise *lesbian*. Still, I push myself to come out whenever it's appropriate and often when it's not: for my own sake and for the sake of women who have more to risk than I do.

My true coming-out story – like that of all lesbians – cannot be told in the past tense. We have yet to see how it ends.

About the Contributors

Angelus (Angela Bowen) is a writer and public speaker who has contributed to a number of newspapers, journals, and anthologies since 1983. Her chapbook *Children in Our Lives: Another View of Lesbians Choosing Children* was published by Profile Productions in 1990. She is now a Ph.D. candidate in women's studies at Clark University in Worcester, Massachusetts. Audre Lorde, the inspiration for her out lesbian life, pointedly addressed her as Angelus, her given name, which she discarded at age twelve and reclaimed at fifty. With Audre gone, she misses hearing it and invites all friends to address her by that name.

Karen Barber is the editor of the erotica collections *Bushfire* and *Afterglow*. She lives in the Boston area.

Nona Caspers's fiction and poetry have appeared in literary journals such as *Calyx, Hurricane Alice,* and *Negative Capability*. Her fiction was featured in *Voyages Out* 2 (with Julie Blackwomon), and her stories have also been anthologized in *Word of Mouth* and *Women on Women* 2. She is the author of the novel *The Blessed,* published by Silverleaf Press.

Alana Corsini in a novelist and poet who has worked as a fund raiser and arts manager for cultural organizations the past fifteen years. She lives in New York City and Sag Harbor, New York.

Emma Joy Crone, no longer celibate, has been enjoying a relationship with a 38-year-old for the past five years. Recently, her writing has included poetry and erotica. She also continues the quest to increase the visibility of old lesbians and has been published in magazines and a British Columbia newspaper. She celebrates her sixty-sixth birthday in 1994.

Susan J. Friedman continues to struggle with coming-out issues on a daily basis. She has published work in *Common Lives, Lesbian Lives,* and *Getting Wet,* and has a story forthcoming in the anthology *Out Rage.* She shares her home in Watertown, Massachusetts, with two feisty felines and a well-loved computer. She is grateful to the members of Ginger Twist for their gentle criticism and loving support.

Sally Miller Gearhart is a lesbian-feminist-activist-writer and retired professor of speech communications. She lives in Northern California and is a student of t'ai chi, yoga, barbershop harmony, and pitbulls.

Jewelle Gomez is the author of the vampire novel *The Gilda Stories* and a collection of essays, *Forty-three Septembers.* Formerly the director of the literature program for the New York State Council on the Arts, she currently lives and teaches in San Francisco.

Gillian Hanscombe is an Australian lesbian poet and writer who has lived in Britain since 1969. She has published poems, articles, stories, and journalism in a variety of anthologies, collections, and periodicals and has given many readings in Britain, North America, and Australia. Her publications include *Between Friends, Rocking the Cradle* (with Jackie Forster), and *Flesh and Paper* (with Suniti Namjoshi). Her most recent book is *Sybil the Glide of Her Tongue,* published by Spinifex Press (Australia) in 1992.

Linda Heal writes, "I'm currently underemployed in Madison, Wisconsin, which is teeming with lesbians and creative haircuts. Recently my lover became my life partner in a ceremony that included lots of music, dancing, trees, and grass. My mom was my best woman."

Sarah Holmes is a political activist and writer who works in publishing and lives with her lover and their cats in the Boston area.

Marcie Just is a resident of Colorado, living on the banks of the Roaring Fork River. She shares her home with her love, Traci, and her three feline companions, Ishi, Sakti, and Gandolf. She is an astrologer, herbalist, and free-lance writer.

Lynn Kanter's novel *On Lill Street* was published in 1992 by Third Side Press. Her work has appeared in *The Time of Our Lives; Confronting Cancer, Constructing Change;* and *Common Lives, Lesbian Lives.* She was a founding member of Virago Video, a women's television production company, and wrote the award-winning ERA documentary *Fighting for the Obvious.* Lynn Lives in Washington, D.C.

Pam McArthur lives in eastern Massachusetts with her lover, Beth; their son, Aaron; and their two aging cats. She spends her time being an at-home mom, riding horses, dreaming of Antarctica, and writing. Through her writing, she celebrates her life and connects with other lesbians — she says it's a struggle sometimes, but it keeps her sane! Her work has appeared in numerous journals and anthologies, including *Bushfire, Afterglow,* and *Out Rage.*

Judith McDaniel lives in Tucson, Arizona, where she is writing *A Lesbian Couples Guide* (HarperCollins, 1995) and teaching communications courses. Her most recent novel, *Just Say Yes* (Firebrand, 1991), is a lesbian romance set in Provincetown.

Toni McNaron is a professor of English and women's studies at the University of Minnesota, where she has taught for the past thirty years. Her publications include *Voices in the Night: Women Speaking about Incest* (co-edited with Yarrow Morgan), *The Sister Bond: A Feminist View of a Timeless Connection, I Dwell in Possibility: A Memoir,* and numerous articles on Virginia Woolf, lesbian pedagogy, Radclyffe Hall, and other lesbian writers. She is currently collecting her unpublished speeches and essays from the past three decades for a book on her own and her university's handling of lesbian and gay issues.

Lesléa Newman is a writer and editor with sixteen books to her credit, including *Heather Has Two Mommies, In Every Laugh a Tear, A Letter to Harvey Milk, Sweet Dark Places,* and *Writing from the Heart: Inspiration and Exercises for Women Who Want to Write.* She makes her home in Northampton, Massachusetts.

Liz O'Lexa is a 26-year-old, long-haired, feminist femme, who is nothing if not completely herself. She divides her time between working, sleeping, writing, and spending quality time with her three cats. She writes erotic love poetry (when properly inspired) and is the author of the play *Do You Still Dance?*

Candyce Rusk is an urban activist who divides her time between Boston and Provincetown. Her writing web includes music, poetry, and fiction.

Karen X. Tulchinsky is a Jewish lesbian political activist and writer who lives in Vancouver, British Columbia, with her lover Suzanne. Her work has appeared in the anthologies *Getting Wet, Lovers, Sister/Stranger, Love's Shadow, Out Rage,* and *Afterglow.* She has stories forthcoming in the anthologies *Breaking Up Is Hard to Do* and *Sister and Brother.*

Nancy Wechsler is a longtime political activist living in Somerville, Massachusetts. Her writings have appeared in *Gay Community News.* Since 1986, she has worked at Resist, a foundation that funds grassroots organizations across the country working toward peace and social justice.

Other books of interest from

ALYSON PUBLICATIONS

AFTERGLOW, edited by Karen Barber, $9.00. With the excitement of new love, the remembrances of past lovers, *Afterglow* offers more well-crafted, imaginative, sexy stories of lesbian desire in the best-selling tradition of *Bushfire*.

BUSHFIRE, edited by Karen Barber, $9.00. Amidst our differences, all lesbians share one thing: a desire for women. Sometimes intensely sexual, other times subtly romantic, this emotion is always incredibly powerful. These short stories celebrate lesbian desire in all its forms.

LESBIAN QUOTATIONS, by Rosemary E. Silva, $10.00. Where are all the quotable lesbians? Author Rosemary Silva has collected the best of lesbian wit and wisdom in one volume, on topics ranging from Passion to Pets.

HAPPY ENDINGS ARE ALL ALIKE, by Sandra Scoppettone, $7.00. It was their last summer before college, and Jaret and Peggy were in love. But as Jaret said, "It always seems as if when something great happens, then something lousy happens soon after."

BI ANY OTHER NAME, edited by Loraine Hutchins and Lani Kaahumanu, $12.00. In this ground-breaking anthology, over seventy women and men from all walks of life describe their lives as bisexuals in prose, poetry, art, and essays.

LESBIAN LISTS, by Dell Richards, $9.00. Fun facts like banned lesbian books, lesbians who've passed as men, black lesbian entertainers, and switch-hitters are sure to amuse and make *Lesbian Lists* a great gift.

THE LESBIAN SEX BOOK, by Wendy Caster, $15.00. Covering topics from age differences to vibrators, anonymous sex to vegetables, this illustrated handbook is perfect for newly out lesbians as well as those who want to discover more about lesbian sexuality.

ONE TEENAGER IN TEN, edited by Ann Heron, $5.00. One teenager in ten is gay. Here, 26 young people from around the country discuss their coming-out experiences. Their words will provide encouragement for other teenagers facing similar experiences.

THE ALYSON ALMANAC, by Alyson Publications, $10.00. *The Alyson Almanac* is the most complete reference book available about the lesbian and gay community — and also the most entertaining. Here are brief biographies of some 300 individuals from throughout history; a report card for every member of Congress; significant dates from our history; addresses and phone numbers for major organizations, periodicals, and hotlines; and much more.

LEAVE A LIGHT ON FOR ME, by Jean Swallow, $10.00. Real life in real time for four San Francisco lesbians: cold coffee in the kitchen, hot sex on the side, with friendships strong enough to pull them all through.

CHOICES, by Nancy Toder, $9.00. In this straightforward, sensitive novel, Nancy Toder conveys the joys — and fears — of a woman coming to terms with her attraction to other women.

SOCIETY AND THE HEALTHY HOMOSEXUAL, by George Weinberg, $8.00. The man who popularized the term *homophobia* examines its causes, and its disastrous but often subtle effect on gay people. He cautions lesbians and gay men against assuming that universal problems such as loneliness stem from their sexual orientation.

BUTCH, by Jay Rayn, $8.00. Michaeline "Mike" Landetti doesn't have a word for what she is, but from the beginning of memory she has played ball with the boys, and fallen in love with the girls.

WORD GAYMES, by Kathleen DeBold, $9.00. Kathleen DeBold has collected her best crossword puzzles and "gaycrostics" from the *Washington Blade* and *Lambda Book Report,* and created a few new mind-benders, to produce the perfect puzzle book for the gay trivia buff.

ONE MILLION STRONG, by Cece Cox, Lisa Means, and Lisa Pope, $18.00. A photographic remembrance, with text, of one of the largest demonstrations in history for gay, lesbian, and bisexual equality.

SUPPORT YOUR LOCAL BOOKSTORE

Most of the books described here are available at your nearest gay or feminist bookstore, and many of them will be available at other bookstores. If you can't get these books locally, order by mail using this form.

Enclosed is $_____ for the following books. (Add $1.00 postage if ordering just one book. If you order two or more, we'll pay the postage.)

1._____

2._____

3._____

name:_____

address:_____

city:_____state:_____zip:_____

ALYSON PUBLICATIONS
Dept. J-52, 40 Plympton St., Boston, MA 02118

After June 30, 1995, please write for current catalog.